"explains the urgency for people to understand Biblical judgments on sin because our beloved nation, steeped in disobedience to God, is ripe for punishment."
Alex McFarland, Apologetics,
North Greenville University, South Carolina

"In these days that can be confusing, we need biblical guidance as to how God judges a wicked land whether Israel or America."
Jerry Vines, former Pastor of
First Baptist Church, Jacksonville, FL,

"As you read of the sins of the past, you will quickly see how America mirrors Israel past."
Johnny Hunt, Pastor
First Baptist Church, Woodstock, GA

"This powerful and convicting book needs to be read by every citizen who is concerned about the future of America."
Ed Hindson
Dean of School of Divinity at Liberty University

"Dr. Neal Jackson gives America and the church a strong warning of coming judgment."
Herb Reavis, Jr., Pastor
North Jacksonville Baptist Church, Jacksonville, Florida

"The content is not the proverbial elephant in the room, because at this point in our history, that elephant is more like a herd of elephants in full charge. It is not our room, but rather our nation, that is under full frontal attack."
Johnny Pope, Pastor,
Christ Church Baptist Fellowship, Houston, TX

"In the world of books, there are many that CAN BE READ, a host of others that SHOULD BE READ, and a rare few that MUST BE READ. *The Coming Destruction of America* is a MUST READ."
Junior Hill, Evangelist, Author

"America is following the doomed footsteps of ancient Israel. For our nation, it is repent or else!"
Tim Lee, Evangelist, Author

"…a measured and compelling comparison between Israel's apostasy and America's godless trajectory. The arguments are sobering. The concerns are convicting. The call to action is clear – repent or perish."
Doug Small, Evangelist, Author

"Neal Jackson describes in a Biblically sound manner the outcome America will surely face if she continues down the slippery slope she is currently on."
David Ring, Evangelist, Author

"*The Coming Destruction of America* is a must read for people that love God and love their country."
Tom Messer, Pastor
Trinity Baptist Church, Jacksonville, FL,

"David's mighty men had an understanding of the times to know what Israel ought to do. *The Coming Destruction of America* displays an understanding of these perilous times to show what America ought to do."
Joe Arthur, Pastor
Harvest Baptist Church, Jonesboro, GA

"The Biblical truths so intelligibly shared should open the eyes and stir the heart of every reader to pray fervently and take a bold stand for our Sovereign God each day."
Gayle Kurdian, President/CEO,
Matlab, Inc.

"The timing of the book is impeccable as we see the day approaching."
Ray Flynn, President
Hanes Consumer Products

"Pastor Jackson clearly defines the parallel paths of rejection and destruction of nations in Scripture to that of the path America is traveling today."
Dale Lambert, CEO,
Randolph Electric

THE COMING DESTRUCTION OF AMERICA

A Biblical Examination of the Judgments of God Upon a Land

Neal Jackson

THE COMING DESTRUCTION OF AMERICA

A BIBLICAL EXAMINATION OF THE JUDGMENTS OF GOD UPON A LAND

DR. NEAL JACKSON

Copyright © 2018 by Truth Publishing

All rights reserved.

No part of this book may be reproduced in any form or by any electronic or mechanical means, including information storage and retrieval systems, without written permission from the author, except for the use of brief quotations in a book review.

All Scripture quotations are from the KJV.

Cover Design: Tracy Lynn

Editing: Patrick Conley, Matthew Barbour, Nolan Lewis

ISBN-13: 978-1-942363-97-2

CONTENTS

Preface	ix
1. America, God Shed His Grace on Thee	1
2. A Sermon for the Nation	18
3. America in the Mirror	36
4. A Disaster Described	52
5. Mr. Amos Goes to Washington	72
6. Katy Bar the Door	96
7. Me, Myself, and I	114
8. God's Prescription for a Sick Society	134
9. Wanted	151
10. Hope for a Hopeless Society	170
Notes	189

PREFACE

I love America. I was raised to love her, and I still do. When the *Star-Spangled Banner* plays, my back straightens, my right hand finds my heart, and my eyes often release a tear or two. I honor the nation I call home and thank God for that privilege.

Yet my love for country has not blinded me to the stark realities of her present condition. Turning on the news or scrolling through social media brings a barrage of reminders that the America I love, the nation built on the principles of biblical Christianity, has slid from that foundation. We are assailed daily with stories of sex scandals, school shootings, street slaughter, racism, drug epidemics, and rampant immorality of every kind. America has become a sin-sick nation.

Sin's shift, from the back alley to main street, is apparent.

Things once condemned as shameful are now endorsed as normal, even preferable, lifestyle expressions. America has abandoned the moral bedrock of her founding. What began as a shining city on a hill, a refuge of hope for the world, now seems bent on mimicking every other sin-ravaged society. Noticeably, the further we fall from our original values, the more our land suffers.

I often preach about the tragic consequences of unrepentant sin for individuals, homes, and even churches. However, as God led me to write this book, I found myself studying the relationships between God and nations. The premier scriptural example is Israel, God's chosen people. Through research, I discovered strong correlations between Israel's historical trends and the current path of the United States. In fact, as my exploration expanded into the records of other Biblical nations, clear patterns emerged of God's dealings with nations, from His own chosen to the most raging heathen. Understanding these patterns unlocks a broader view of America's unfolding future.

Will we flourish? Will we be destroyed? Is the future bright or bleak? No need for guesswork. God's Word holds the answers.

AMERICA, GOD SHED HIS GRACE ON THEE

It was a cold December day in 1927. The Coast Guard destroyer *"Paulding"* was on a routine patrol off Cape Cod. The day's route would happen to pass through an area used by the Navy for submarine trial runs. On this day, however, it would be no cause for concern for the *Paulding's* crew, for the white and red flag signaling a submarine in the area was not flying. In their minds smooth sailing lay ahead.

Unbeknownst to the crew, and yet to be updated on their charts, the Navy had ended the use of the signal flag for submarine operations. Also, unknown to the *Paulding* crew, a submerged submarine stretched directly across their path with only its periscopes above the surface. The covert design of the submarine, combined with the choppy seas, concealed the wake of the periscope. The *Paulding's* lookouts did not see the danger until it was far too late.

Shortly after three o'clock p.m., two days after Christmas, the *USS Paulding* rammed the starboard side of the United States submarine *S-4*. The *S-4* was instantly crippled, her bow smashed. Rescue operations immediately began as the submarine plunged into total darkness. Lifeboats were lowered from the *Paulding* and divers leaped into action. Reports returned with the outlook bleak; thirty-four of the forty souls on board had perished. Optimism glimmered, however, when word came that six submariners were alive, but trapped inside the descending craft. They communicated with their would-be-rescuers by tapping out Morse code on the hull.

"Is there any hope?"

Their message pleaded for some reason to avoid despair.

"Is there any hope?"

The severe weather continued to hamper the rescue operations.

"Is there any hope?"

The oxygen supply waned.

"Is there any hope?"

The tapping fell silent. The oxygen had run out. The rescue operation became a salvage mission. Forty souls passed into eternity.

Those trapped men have departed this life, but their question lives on. Today, it is not tapped on the hull of a sunken submarine, but spoken across dinner tables, in Sunday School classes, at political rallies, and whispered in almost faithless prayer. "Is there any hope?" we ask. "Is there any hope for America?"

One truth must be known at the onset of this reading. I believe firmly with resounding biblical assurance, there is hope for America. All is not lost. Hope yet remains. That hope remains if America will return to following God and obeying His commandments. Yet, this hope is not a hope of trapped, helpless desperation. This faith is a hope of action. Action that is on the part of God and on the part of a nation.

THE ACCEPTANCE OF GOD AS A PREREQUISITE

The pages of Scripture are filled with promises. There are promises between God and individuals as well as promises between God and groups of individuals, including nations. God operates in covenant promises, and His promises are faithful, whether personal or national. Among the national promises found in Scripture is an assurance that God will bless a nation that declares Jehovah to be their God.

Blessed is the nation whose God is the Lord; *And the people whom he hath chosen for his own inheritance.*

— PSALM 33:12

At first reading this promise is incredible assurance for a nation. Perhaps the most amazing part of this promise is that the word *nation* actually refers to a nation foreign to the author, a Gentile nation. There are few thoughts that could be more radical for a Jewish writer in this time period. This vision was a revolutionary concept that a Gentile nation could experience the blessing of God if only it would turn to Jehovah and yield to Him as Lord.

God's promise extends to any nation that steps into a covenant relationship with Him. A nation or people group experiences the divine blessing of God if they turn to Him in faith and obedience. Communist China will be blessed if they turn to God in repentance and faith. God's benevolent hand will touch Cuba, Libya, Iran, Iraq, and any other nation that turns to Him, seeks His purpose, follows His plan, and obeys His commands.

This eternal decree means that a nation's view of God directly correlates to its national wellbeing. The promise written by the Psalmist speaks of a nation being blessed by placing God in a preeminent position in their society. A nation doing so would consider God and His will in their social milieu, as well as in their governmental decisions. This concept connects to America's heritage, for this is exactly what occurred in our founding. No nation in history, since Israel, began with such Godly intentions. The forefathers of America sowed seeds of devotion to God, and this nation continues to reap the harvest of blessing from their wise choices.

In 1620, when the Pilgrims arrived in America, they were faced with the daunting task of creating a government for their new land. They began by drafting the Mayflower Compact, a document which opens with the words, "In the name of God." It goes on to define the signers' purpose for coming to this new land as being for "the Glory of God and the advancement of Christian faith."[1] Forty-one signers committed to what would be the groundwork for their fledgling society, but not before being reminded by the Compact's own words that their signing was done "in the presence of God."

The Mayflower Compact may have been the first, but it was not the only, nor even the most famous, document from America's founding that sought to affirm God's preeminence in the United States. The Declaration of Independence begins with the words "We hold these truths to be self-evident." In today's language, the writers are saying the truths in the document are obvious. The Declaration goes on to state, "that all men are created equal; that they are endowed by their Creator with certain unalienable rights." The founders made plain that rights are given by God, not government. Governments simply recognize God-given rights. In doing so, they acknowledge that God is the creator. Also included in the Declaration are phrases like "appealing to the Supreme Judge of the world for the rectitude of our intentions" and "with a firm reliance on the protection of divine Providence." These certainly do not sound like the musings of men wishing to launch a secular society. This document was not just a Declaration of Independence from the throne of King George III, it was a declaration of dependence upon the throne of God.

John Hancock was one of the most famous signers of the Declaration of Independence, if only for His unique signature. As plain as his autograph, however, was his view of God. In the face of imminent attack by the British, he reportedly proclaimed, "We recognize no sovereign but God, and no King but Jesus."[2]

James Madison, the architect of the United States Constitution and the fourth president of the United States, was quoted as saying,

> "We have staked the whole future of American civilization not upon the power of government, far from it. We have staked the future of all our political institutions upon the capacity of mankind for self-government, upon the capacity of each and all of us

to govern ourselves, to control ourselves, to sustain ourselves according to the Ten Commandments."[3]

I daresay President Madison would view modern America with great disappointment. Imagine what he would think about a nation removing the Ten Commandments from its schools, lest their religious teaching be offensive. Sadly, his understanding of God's place in morality was prophetic in the aftermath of God's expulsion from public education. The result was a moral decay that has caved into utter depravity. No stone tablets can be found on school premises, but the police are there, daily dealing with the dramatic increase in drugs, crime, and violence. Perhaps we can all agree with President Madison that we would prefer the Commandments to the world that came in their absence.

America's fourth president was not the only early president to speak of God. In fact, George Washington spoke the words "it would be peculiarly improper to omit in this first official Act, my fervent supplications to that Almighty Being" during the first-ever inauguration speech. In that same address, he continued, "we ought to be no less persuaded that the propitious smiles of Heaven, can never be expected on a nation that disregards the eternal rules of order and right, which Heaven itself has ordained."[4]

Washington was also known to speak of God when giving orders to his troops. He ordered the military to conduct church services on Sunday during the Revolutionary War. Washington left no question about his feelings regarding religion in America when he stated, "While we are zealously performing the duties of good citizens and soldiers, we certainly ought not to be inattentive to the higher duties of religion. To the distinguished character of Patriot, it should be our highest glory to add the more distinguished character of Christian."[5] This statement was not simply a matter of rhetoric for Washington. He was well-known for his dependence upon prayer. It is ever so fitting that one of the most famous paintings of him is Arnold Friberg's, *The Prayer at Valley Forge*.

Presidents and generals are not the only ones who held such a view. Daniel Webster served as a congressman, senator, and Secretary of State for three administrations. He was also a man that held Christianity and the Bible in the highest regard. He said, "let us not forget the religious character of our origin. Our fathers were brought hither by their high veneration for the Christian religion. They journeyed by its light and labored in its hope. They sought to incorporate its principles with the elements of their society, and to diffuse its influence through all their institutions, civil, political, or literary."[6] He felt that this incorporation of the Christian religion was of the utmost importance. Webster lamented the probable future of a nation which neglected the Bible, saying

"If religious books are not widely circulated among

the masses in this country, I do not know what is going to become of us as a nation. If truth be not diffused, error will be; If God and His Word are not known and received, the devil and his works will gain the ascendancy; If the evangelical volume does not reach every hamlet, the pages of a corrupt and licentious literature will; If the power of the Gospel is not felt throughout the length and breadth of the land, anarchy, and misrule, degradation, and misery, corruption, and darkness will reign without mitigation or end."[7]

We now live in a world where the separation of church and state often becomes a club to beat down any Christian ideology that dares raise its voice in the public sector. Again and again, secular voices shut down anyone who speaks from a Judeo-Christian worldview. Forgetting the many positives that this worldview has brought to western culture, they act as if anyone speaking from a Christian perspective is an enemy of the state that must be silenced.

Yet those who would silence the influence of the church upon the state would do well to remember the words of John Quincy Adams, sixth president of the United States: "the highest glory of the American Revolution was this: It connected in one indissoluble bond the principles of civil government with the principles of Christianity."[8] Echoing Adams' sentiments was his successor to the presidency, who said, "The Bible is the rock upon which our republic stands."[9] This observation isn't the words of some fiery tent revivalist nor a stern pulpiteer, but of Andrew Jackson our seventh president.

There are few presidents with the lasting impact or respect than that of Abraham Lincoln. He, like many of his predecessors, was known to be a man of faith. In 1861, bidding farewell to his hometown of Springfield, Illinois, Lincoln stated, "I go to assume a task more difficult than that which devolved upon Washington. Unless the great God, who assisted him, shall be with me and aid me, I must fail; but if the same omniscient mind and almighty arm that directed and protected him shall guide and support me, I shall not fail."[10] It was evident that Lincoln believed the success of the nation and her president was a direct result of dependence upon God.

This idea, that seeking God brings blessing, as spoken by the Psalmist, is alive and well in America. Roger Babson, the famed business theorist and economist of the early 20th century, once noted the difference between North America and South America in prosperity. While visiting a South American president, he recalls a conversation that turned to the fact that, despite its abundant resources, South America greatly lags behind North America economically. The leader explained that while those who settled South America had come seeking gold, the settlers of North America had come seeking God. His belief was that America's unique founding purpose was the catalyst for its prosperity.

There can be no doubt that America is unique in her willingness to accept God as the prerequisite of any nation's success. No other nation has "In God We Trust" printed on its currency. No other nation has a chaplain open in prayer when its legislative bodies are in session. No other nation, since Israel, has the spiritual heritage of following God from its founding. When one views American prosperity in the light of God's promises, it becomes obvious. The prosperity of the United States is not a matter of luck, but of the Lord. America's blessing is a direct result of the promise that a covenant-keeping God will reward righteous nations.

ACCOUNTABILITY TO GOD AS A PRIORITY

> *The LORD looketh from heaven; He beholdeth all the sons of men. From the place of his habitation he looketh Upon all the inhabitants of the earth. He fashioneth their hearts alike; He considereth all their works.*
>
> — PSALM 33:13-15

It is impossible to accept the idea of a Sovereign God

without submitting to His authority. The United States of America has declared its dependence upon God on its currency and in its national motto. It only follows that a God worthy of a nation's trust ought to be respected and feared. Jehovah God is not only our greatest hope. He is our greatest threat. Yes, He has promised to bless the nation that follows Him, but He promises to judge the nation that rebels against Him.

When a nation condones the murder of millions of babies each year, endorses homosexuality as an acceptable lifestyle, removes the Ten Commandments from schoolrooms and courtrooms, forbids prayer at public school gatherings, and assaults the Christian freedoms of its citizens, that nation has a problem. It has forgotten the spiritual foundation upon which it was built.

The Scriptures teach that God hates the shedding of innocent blood. Yet in America, a doctor that murders a child in his mother's womb is rewarded financially. The politicians and judges who allow and promote these murders are applauded as progressive thinkers for giving the mother a choice. Meanwhile, destroying the egg of an eagle can result in thousands of dollars of fines and incarceration. What a forthcoming sign of the times! One thing is certain; a nation that destroys its own babies will know the judgment of Almighty God in the near future.

It has been said that the wheels of justice turn slowly, but they are always turning. The same announcement could be said of God's wrath. We must not think that God condones our nation's actions simply because we have not seen fire falling from Heaven. America is already experiencing the withdrawal of God's blessings. The land, once viewed as the greatest, most powerful, most revered nation on the face of the earth, has become a laughingstock to many countries who oppose us and our positions. The shining city on a hill now has more trouble than many of its neighbors.

Every day in America, tens of thousands of people are raped, mugged, or robbed on our streets. Every day in America, hundreds of babies are born addicted to drugs. Every day in America, thousands of children quit school. Every day in America, the national debt increases by billions. Every day in America, hundreds of U.S. companies file for bankruptcy.

Every night much of the population of our country sits glued to televisions, computers, and phone screens. They watch all sorts of violence, adultery, perversion, and witchcraft. Despite knowing the damage that is being done, they call it entertainment. Meanwhile, they wonder why the United States has one of the highest rates of divorce and addiction in the world. This fact should not be a surprise. When a nation approves what God forbids, there is always consequences. America has chosen to hide its Christian history in the closet and deny the authority of God as the basis of right and wrong. In so doing, America has forfeited God's blessings for His judgment.

America is forcing the hand of God. God must either judge America or abdicate His position as a holy and just God. As Billy Graham said, "If God doesn't judge America for her sin, He will owe Sodom and Gomorrah an apology." America is sick. If something does not change, we will join the graveyard of the nations because of our rebellion against God and His ways.

One of the inscriptions on the Jefferson Memorial, taken from Jefferson's own words, captures this truth: "God who gave us life gave us liberty. Can the liberties of a nation be secure when we have removed a conviction that these liberties are the gift of God? Indeed I tremble for my country when I reflect that God is just and that his justice cannot sleep forever."[11]

GOD'S ASSISTANCE AS A PRIORITY

> [16] There is no king saved by the multitude of an host: A mighty man is not delivered by much strength. [17] An horse is a vain thing for safety: Neither shall he deliver any by his great strength. [18] Behold, the eye of the LORD is upon them that fear him, Upon them that hope in his mercy; [19] To deliver their soul from death, And to keep them alive in famine.

> *²⁰Our soul waiteth for the* LORD: *He is our help and our shield.*
>
> — PSALM 33:16–20

Some ideologies propose government as the answer to a nation's problems. However, I submit that government, without God, is the problem in America. When a government abandons God, it seeks to take the place of God by controlling men's lives and welfare. While I believe that there are some in government sincerely trying to help improve our country, I also understand that neither Congress nor the White House can solve the nation's problems. Only God can.

Another voice in our nation cries, not for deliverance from Government, but from gold. These people believe that the answer to all of our woes is economic, and that societal problems are caused by poverty, not immorality. For this crowd, the answer is simply to grow the economy. Unfortunately, they fail to understand that a wealthy, unregenerate heart is no better morally than a poor, unregenerate heart. There is no financial solution to a spiritual and moral problem.

America does not need government to save her. She cannot be redeemed by an economic resurgence. America needs God. He alone is the solution to her problems. This concept must be more than theory. The church must trumpet this reality: there can be no redemption or restoration without returning to God. As Woodrow Wilson said, "Our civilization cannot survive materially unless it is redeemed spiritually. It can be saved only by becoming permeated with the Spirit of Christ and being made free and happy by practices which spring out of that spirit. Only thus can discontent be driven out and all shadows lifted from the road ahead."[12]

America needs leaders like Moses who are determined to obey God and seek His glory. America needs generals like Joshua who know God and can pray things into reality. America needs politicians like Joseph who walk with God and seek His will in every matter. America needs preachers like Peter who look people in the eye and denounce their sin. America needs mothers like Hannah who pray for their children and give them to God, raising them according to His commands. America needs children like Samuel who talk with God in hours of the night and honor their parents in the hours of the day. America needs physicians like Luke who care for the physical and spiritual needs of their patients. America needs a church, like the New Testament church, that seeks God's will and lives by His word. America needs God.

Perhaps the greatest sermon about this need came not from a pulpit but from President Franklin D. Roosevelt's radio address on the 23rd of February, 1936. His statement has grown more true as time has passed;

"No greater thing could come to our land today than a revival of the spirit of religion — a revival that would sweep through the homes of the Nation and stir the hearts of men and women of all faiths to a reassertion of their belief in God and their dedication to His will for themselves and for their world. I doubt if there is any problem social, political, or economic—that would not melt away before the fire of such a spiritual awakening."[13]

A SERMON FOR THE NATION

One broadcast that captures my interest each year is the State of the Union Address. Anticipation swells as the President of the United States takes the podium to deliver his thoughts on the wellbeing of the country and the challenges she faces. The nation's Executive addresses both the United States Senate and the House of Representatives, as well as the Supreme Court. I may not agree with the sitting President's political philosophy or party affiliation, but for me, the State of the Union is must-see TV. It is a healthy practice for a leader to stand before his people and give an account of the nation's position in the present and posture for the future.

This tradition is not a new one. In fact, a speech much like the State of the Union can be read in the Bible. In the eighth chapter of Deuteronomy, Moses addresses the Israelites as they prepare to enter the Promised Land. After four decades of wandering in the wilderness, the nation was poised for a period of war and settlement in her new home. Also imminent was a leadership transition, as Moses would be replaced by his protege, a young general named Joshua. I can imagine the scene. The crowd buzzes with commentary, perhaps some calling Moses a "lame duck" leader as Joshua takes the stage. He looks into the faces of a people he has led for the equivalent of ten presidential terms, clears his throat, and begins to speak. His address bears the tone of authority, but also a heartfelt plea that they would honor and obey God in all they do. This is not just a speech, this is an impassioned sermon to his nation, one to which America would be wise to heed.

GOD'S REQUIREMENT FOR A NATION

> *Therefore thou shalt keep the commandments of the LORD thy God, to walk in his ways, and to fear him.*
>
> — DEUTERONOMY 8:6

As Moses begins his address, he quickly develops a theme of response to Jehovah's bidding. Three times in the chapter, he repeats the message of submitting to God's commands. He tells the people to "keep the commandments." The word *keep* here carries more significance than simply following orders. It means to watch over, to guard, protect, promote, and obey.

God's people are to keep a diligent eye upon His commands and obey them faithfully. This defensive stance protects us from sin. Far too many believers never experience victory and never become all that God has called them to become because they have areas of disobedience in their lives. The person who keeps a diligent watch upon the preeminence of God's commands in his life will find himself acting upon them. Moses does not call for Israel to *keep* God's commands in a passive sense. Rather, he instructs them to actively prioritize the directives of God in every area of their life. In the same spirit that led him to ask "Shew me now thy way," Moses reminds the people that keeping the commandments of God will cause them to walk in obedience to His ways.

To walk in God's ways is to go in His direction, or to follow His plan. When facing life's choices and unknown circumstances, the believer must ask, "Which way leads to God?" The evidence of a person's respect and reverence for God can be seen in his walk. The God-focused walk is characterized, not by fear of going astray, but by a confidence in knowing that each step is ordained by the Almighty, Himself.

On the other hand, a life lived in rebellion to the principles found in Scripture follows and unguided, unguarded path.

Only a fool expects God's blessings on a life that refuses to obey His clear commands. For those whose desired destination is peace and purpose, God has provided a detailed route – obedience to Him and His Word.

In John 14, Jesus says, "If ye love me, keep my commandments." He is saying that your obedience to His commands is the foremost measurement of your affection for Him. The goal of God's commands is to bring the Christian into a close relationship with Him. A man's love for his wife is a perfectly adequate reason to reject the advances of another woman. In the same way, a Christian's love for God is a perfectly good reason to reject Satan's seduction. A great example of this principle is found with Joseph. Potiphar's wife attempts to allure him, but he rejects her advances by saying, "How then can I do this great wickedness, and sin against God?" His love for God resulted in a pure and holy life.

Moses instructs the people to keep God's commandments and to walk in His ways, but he also includes an admonition to fear God. Fearing the Lord is a consistent Biblical theme. Psalm 111 says, "The fear of the LORD *is* the beginning of wisdom: a good understanding have all they that do *his commandments*." Proverbs 1:7 says, "The fear of the LORD *is* the beginning of knowledge: b*ut* fools despise wisdom and instruction." The fear of God is the foundation of the life of any believer. It is impossible to truly know God without a proper fear and respect for Him.

You cannot obey an order that you do not understand. Thus, we must truly grasp what it means to fear God. When we fear Him, we have deep and enduring respect for Him and His ways. It is a desire to please Him above all. It is a reverence for God and His holiness that compels us to avoid anything that will hurt Him or impede His working. Fearing God is not trembling before an angry, vindictive being in the sky who is eager to crush you. Rather, fearing God is a posture of humility in the heart that leads one to a reverent desire to honor Him. The fear of God leads to a life of daily obedience to His will.

> *fearing God is a posture of humility in the heart that leads one to a reverent desire to honor Him.*

The principles laid out by Moses are the very ideals upon which the United States was founded. George Bancroft, in his 1866 work, *History of the United States*, quotes Benjamin Franklin: "He who shall introduce into public affairs the principles of primitive Christianity will change the face of the world."[1] John Adams, our second president said, "The destiny of America is to carry the gospel of Jesus Christ to all men."[2] It is surreal to see that a nation founded upon the respect and reverence for God reject any form of God's influence on her course. What was the basis for our democracy is now despised and ridiculed by those who have enjoyed her many blessings.

GOD'S REWARD FOR A NATION

> *For the LORD thy God bringeth thee into a good land, a land of brooks of water, of fountains and depths that spring out of valleys and hills;*
>
> — DEUTERONOMY 8:7

A good leader understands the best results come from people who have been inspired, not merely required to do a certain task. Moses understood this principle and was careful to explain the benefits of pursuing the ideals that he described. The result of Israel keeping God's commandments and reverencing Him is tangible. In response to their reverence and obedience, God blessed them with a land of their own. Furthermore, this possession would not be just any land, but a good land, full of natural resources, flowing with brooks of water, fountains, and springs of abundance. This land would be a pleasant, picturesque, and peaceful place. Their land would be blessed beyond imagination because of their obedience.

Nations are always blessed for their reverence to God. America is no exception. The United States is not a perfect nation, but she is the closest thing today to what could be called a Christian nation. Dr. Ben Carson, world-renowned neurosurgeon, and Housing Secretary once said, "I already won the lottery. I was born in America and I know the Lord." I concur with Dr. Carson. If you were born in the United States, you should count yourself blessed beyond measure. You could have been born in a country where Islam is the primary religion, but you were born in America!

Our forefathers came here to found a Christian nation. They wanted a society where they could openly worship God without fear of persecution, and as we saw in the last chapter, they believed Christianity should be at the forefront of our culture and government. As a result of our obedience to God's way, we have been the beneficiaries of many of the same blessings that Israel enjoyed.

> *A land of wheat, and barley, and vines, and fig trees, and pomegranates; a land of oil olive, and honey;*
>
> — DEUTERONOMY 8:8

Hundreds of years before Moses' address, a man named Jacob took his family to Egypt in order to escape a famine. Amazingly, considering they were fleeing famine, his family flourished in Egypt. Seeing their growing numbers, and fearing a group of foreigners would become too powerful, Egypt's ruler forced them to be slaves. For four hundred years they were under the whip of their masters, but in Deuteronomy God brings them into a land that is their own.

In economics, goods are often discussed by scarcity. Scarcity occurs when there is a natural limit to the possible supply of goods. Scarcity, through supply and demand, raises the value and desirability for a good. In our lives we may not be economists, but we understand scarcity. Have you ever had a "good" Hot Pocket? You know, those meat and cheese-filled microwavable pastries. When you compare them with the cuisine of a well-trained chef or the home cooking of your mother, Hot Pockets just are not all that tasty. Yet, at times you may have spent many hours without food, so hungry you wonder if you will survive the necessary three minutes to heat that lava-filled biscuit. In those moments, you have absolutely enjoyed a food that is mediocre at best.

Just like a mediocre meal seems extraordinary after a long day without eating, any place of freedom would seem like emancipation to a slave. Even so, God does not just give them a parcel of real estate. He promises a land full of wonderful foods from wheat and barley for bread, to vines, figs, and pomegranates for fruit. After centuries of working for the gain of others, God now brings them into a land where provisions are waiting for their arrival. What a turnaround! What a blessed people!

America understands the incredible benefits of God's blessing. To say God is good to America would be a terrible understatement of reality. We have all kinds of fruits, oils, breads, meats, vegetables, and desserts. In fact, with an annual total of over $100 billion, the United States is the world's largest exporter of agricultural goods. Most Americans eat three meals a day (a luxury in many parts of the world), and have cupboards full of snack items for consumption between those meals. Our nation is so blessed that weight loss experts warn against "boredom eating." Our refrigerators are full and our shelves running over. Do you realize how much we have been blessed by God?

> *A land wherein thou shalt eat bread without scarceness, thou shalt not lack any thing in it; a land whose stones are iron, and out of whose hills thou mayest dig brass.*
>
> — DEUTERONOMY 8:9

Food is necessary for survival, but it takes more than food for a nation to thrive. Thankfully, God never runs short on provisions for the righteous! Not only would Israel eat bread without shortage, they would also have an abundance of other resources. They would have as much iron, brass, and copper as they needed. These resources would enable them to fashion tools, build cities, and forge weapons for protection.

The United States knows this blessing as well. For decades America has carried the reputation of being the strongest country in the world, both economically and militarily. Natural resources like fertile soil, vast forests, oil, natural gas, coal, iron, and an abundance of minerals provide for the needs (and wants) of America's citizens. Yet another blessing is our water supply. While much of the world suffers from the effects of polluted water, we have an abundant supply of pure water for our consumption. Additionally, the United States military is by far the most powerful in the world, allowing these blessings to be enjoyed with a sense of security and safety.

America is exceedingly blessed. In terms of wealth and resources, it could easily be argued that God has given us more than He gave the nation of Israel. From resources to climate to position on the map, God has smiled upon America. This knowledge ought to render us a nation of constant worshipers. Sadly, we are so busy enjoying the blessings of God that we fail to spend time thanking Him for those blessings.

> *When thou hast eaten and art full, then thou shalt bless the* L ORD *thy God for the good land which he hath given thee.*
>
> — DEUTERONOMY 8:10

Moses uses language that is unfamiliar to us. We are quite accustomed to speaking of God blessing His people but are often unfamiliar with the concept of God being blessed. This is due to a misunderstanding of the word *bless* that

Moses uses. Here the word describes kneeling as an act of worship or praise. Israel was among the smallest nations in the entire region. Yet, they found themselves blessed because God protected and promoted them with His supernatural power. Moses determines that his people will maintain an attitude of gratitude for God's favor upon their land.

America would do well to follow the words of Moses. We ought to adore, praise, and thank God for all of His goodness in our lives. We ought to bless Him by bowing before Him. Do not forget, when we honor the Lord, we invite Him to continue as our provider and protector! The greatest army in the world is no comparison for the defense afforded by the hand of God. When we look at the goodness of God to this nation, we ought to shout His praises constantly, never ceasing to thank Him for all He has done. It would also do us well to remember that a nation possesses no more gratitude as a whole than that which is possessed by each individual citizens. Each person that receives God's blessing has a responsibility to express appreciation for His mercy and blessings.

GOD'S REMEMBRANCE BY A NATION

*Beware that thou forget not the L*ORD *thy God, in not keeping* *his commandments, and his judgments, and his statutes, which I command thee this day:*

— DEUTERONOMY 8:11

Have you noticed that you most need God when you need God? From another angle it could be said that our prioritization of God is often directly related to our need at the moment. In the midst of hardship, we are quick to call upon God, yet we quickly push Him aside when our situation changes for the better. How many times have you found yourself neglecting God when everything was going well, only to realize how far from Him you were in your moment of need?

Moses' great concern for his people was that this blessing-induced forgetfulness did not take up residence in the hearts of Israel. In the wilderness, they had depended upon Jehovah-Jireh, God the provider. He had supplied their food, set their course, guided their leader, and sent their law. God had provided everything for them, and now Moses warns them not to forget Him when they entered the land of promise.

"Well, Rock, let's put it this way. Three years ago you were supernatural. You was hard and nasty. You had this cast iron jaw. But then, the worst thing happened to you that could happen to any fighter. You got civilized."

That line was spoken by fictional boxer Rocky Balboa's

trainer Mickey. In the conversation, Rocky is trying to convince his longtime friend and trainer that he is capable of fighting Clubber Lang, but Mickey is trying to protect Rocky from what he thinks will be a very bad night for his friend. Rocky cannot understand why Mickey no longer believes in him, and Mickey responds by speaking the truth to the fighter. Good times had stolen Rocky's hunger and dulled his edge. He was no longer as tough as he once was because he no longer needed to be tough. No longer the scrappy underdog, now he had some money, a family, and fame. Rocky had forgotten what lack was all about.

This very same detriment, forgetting lack, was what Moses feared would happen to Israel. In the promised land they would have an abundance of food and water. He knew that if they were not intentional about remembering what God had done, they would become complacent with their blessing. How strange it is that the blessings of God have a tendency to lead the very recipients of these blessings to a place of forgetfulness of Who it is that blesses them in the first place. Understand, forgetting God does not mean that we no longer remember that He exists. Forgetting God means we no longer have Him as the first priority in our life. This forgetfulness is dangerous because it leads to a neglect of His ways and disobedience of His commands.

There is a tendency to take God's goodness for granted. Israel was often guilty of this sin. They thought since they were God's chosen people, they could live however they pleased without suffering any consequences. How often do today's Christians find themselves falling into the same way of thinking? We revel in the blessings of God but neglect the God of the blessings. Like Israel (and like Rocky) we get complacent and presumptuous. We seem to forget we need God, and start acting like God can't make it without us! We could not be more wrong or foolish.

When compared with other nations, America's 1776 birth date makes her a relatively young country. At just over 240 years old, we are young by history's standards. Yet, for those two and a half centuries, God has greatly blessed our country. Unfortunately, like Israel so often did, America has seemed to forget where our blessings are derived.

America has forgotten God. We need to look no further than the daily news to see this. There are groups trying to remove *under God* from our pledge. Other groups are seeking to remove *In God We Trust* from our currency. These are examples that we have forgotten God. Sexual activists are encouraging all manner of deviants to "come out and go public," all the while Bible-believing Christians are told to hold their tongue and lay down their God-given beliefs. Under the constant threat of being called bigots, Christians are repeatedly told to be tolerant of sin. Meanwhile, sinners are free to prosecute us for our beliefs.

> [12]*Lest when thou hast eaten and art full, and hast built goodly houses, and dwelt therein;* [13]*And when thy herds and thy flocks*

multiply, and thy silver and thy gold is multiplied, and all that thou hast is multiplied;

— DEUTERONOMY 8:12-13

Moses warns Israel of their prosperity dulling their spirituality. He speaks of food. America has an abundance of food while many around the world are starving. He speaks of their nice homes. If you have a roof over your head, you should count yourself blessed. In America, we have palatial estates in comparison to the rest of the world. If you ever visit a third world country, you will quickly realize why so many people are sacrificing so much to come to America. In fact, you cannot turn on the news any day without hearing about immigration issues. There is a reason the world wants to live here, we have been greatly blessed by God.

Continuing with his recitation of their blessings, Moses speaks of their livestock. They had many sheep, goats, cattle, and oxen. They, like America, were blessed with an abundance of agricultural wealth. He speaks of their silver and gold, their money. In America, we are blessed to have checking accounts, stocks, and retirement funds. How often do you thank God for your monthly statement or the balance on your banking app? Whatever the amount of your material blessings, you should take care to thank God for it. He has blessed you with all that you have.

> *Then thine heart be lifted up, and thou forget the Lord thy God, which brought thee forth out of the land of Egypt, from the house of bondage;*
>
> — DEUTERONOMY 8:14

Now Moses comes to the fruit of forgetting God, pride. The insidious thing about pride is that it leads to flesh-centered, self-pleasing, and totally debauched living. Pride destroys a person as they go further into gratifying their own desires and get farther and farther from pleasing God. The same is true of a nation.

The Psalmist wrote, "The wicked shall be turned into hell and all the nations that forget God."

America is living out this reality. The United States now leads the industrialized world in murder, rape, and violent crime. Worldwide, human trafficking generates tens of billions in annual revenue, and Americans are among its leading subsidizers. America spends well over $20 billion a year feeding its porn habit. This number is small when compared to the $100 billion-plus Americans spend on illegal (not to mention abuse of legal) drugs each year. Perhaps, America needs drugs to dull its conscience. No nation with an intact moral compass can accept New York's decision to recognize NAMBLA (the North American Man-Boy Love Association, an organization for pedophiles) as a legitimate non-profit organization. This shocking acceptance means that this group that exists for the purpose of promoting pedophilia can receive the same benefits, protections, and tax exemptions as a soup kitchen, homeless shelter, the United Way, Salvation Army, or even your local church. There can be no denying, any nation that promotes such wickedness has long forgotten God.

GOD'S REPROOF OF A NATION

> [19]And it shall be, if thou do at all forget the LORD thy God, and walk after other gods, and serve them, and worship them, I testify against you this day that ye shall surely perish. [20]As the nations which the LORD destroyeth before your face, so shall ye perish; because ye would not be obedient unto the voice of the LORD your God.
>
> — DEUTERONOMY 8:19-20

God is a God of covenants and His word is reliable. He promises blessings if a nation serves Him, but He also warns that straying nations will suffer the consequences of their choices. Through Moses, God "testifies" or states a solemn promise that if they forget Him, if they turn to other gods, they will perish. Moses reminds them of the nations that they have witnessed God destroy. It was important they let those events be a reminder that God will not spare the disobedient.

This passage is more than a warning to Israel. It is also a wake-up call for America. If countries throughout history have experienced destruction for rebellion against God, how can we expect any less? Recall the words of Billy Graham that were quoted in chapter one when he spoke of God needing to apologize to Sodom if America escapes judgment. When other nations turned from God's ways, they met destruction. If we do the same, we should expect the same.

If you look for signs of America's fall, you will not have to look far. Dr. J.D. Unwin, an English social anthropologist studied the birth and death of 80 civilizations, and the same pattern was evident in each of them. Each civilization Dr. Unwin studied fell following the breakdown of the family and a rise in societal immorality. As the moral milieu worsened, social energy abated, resulting in the decay (if not complete destruction) of that civilization.

Many books and articles are written comparing the United States to the Roman Empire. Both nations rose to levels of power and influence that were far superior that of their contemporaries. Yet, as we know, Rome collapsed. Could it be that America is on the brink of the same epitaph?

AMERICA IN THE MIRROR

When God moves, He rarely does so by some apparent force of nature. There are occasions where He intervenes through weather, or an earthquake, or fire falling from the sky, but in the majority of scriptural accounts, God's acts are far less conspicuous. Rather, God works through men and women who willingly submit to His calling and direction. Through these agents, God operates to bring about His will on Earth. Throughout history, we see God worked through human agents, both individuals and nations, to further His purposes. Interestingly, in modern history, God has chosen the same agent again and again to accomplish His plans.

Who was God's agent to stop Hitler and his SS troops? Who did God use to stop the advance of atheistic communism around the globe? What nation did God summon to end the murderous reign of Saddam Hussein? What country's military hunted down Osama Bin Laden? What nation is holding back Iran, Syria, North Korea, and the rise of an Islamic Caliphate? What country has been called upon again and again to stand against the rise of one evil after another? The answer to all these questions is the United States of America.

God has blessed America. Knowing this, the biblical principles "freely ye have received, freely give," and "for unto whomsoever much is given, of him shall be much required," should always be remembered. God has not blessed America merely for America's sake; He has blessed America to bless the world. Sadly, America has forgotten from whence she is blessed. She has forgotten her God.

She is not alone in her backsliding. The book of II Chronicles tells of the destruction of Judah, along with Jerusalem, her capital. The account details how a nation, once blessed by God, can find itself made desolate by His wrath. Most alarming are the many parallels between Israel and our nation. As already discussed, America has been incredibly favored by God. Yet, now we see God being pushed out of every facet of her society. What happened to Israel can happen to America if she repeats their mistakes. America should consider herself warned.

You have probably seen a list of great leaders on the internet or in a magazine. Every time a president is discussed, the conversation inevitably turns to how he ranks in relation to his predecessors. Depending on the political leanings of those doing the ranking, the results vary widely. However, when it comes to God's opinion, only one criteria matters; was this a godly or ungodly ruler?

As a nation, Israel had godly and ungodly leaders, many times close together. In 597 BC, Zedekiah, the youngest son of King Josiah, became the king of Israel. Unfortunately for Israel, Zedekiah was nothing like his father. Josiah had followed God, but his son lived a wicked life. Despite the counsel of God's prophet, Jeremiah, Zedekiah refused to heed God's word. He became known as a king that "did that which was evil in the sight of the Lord." This action would cost Israel dearly.

In the years before Zedekiah took the throne, a city-state known as Babylon had begun to increase in power, wealth, and influence. In 612 BC, this rising nation defeated Assyria, solidifying its place as a superpower. Unsatisfied, Babylon went on to defeat Egypt in 605 BC. The global juggernaut soon collided with Israel, conquering Jerusalem and hauling back to Babylon thousands of captives including Daniel, Hananiah, Mishael, and Azariah. The latter three would become famous by their Babylonian names, Shadrach, Meshach, and Abednego.

In 597 BC, there was unrest in Jerusalem, and Nebuchadnezzar, Babylon's ruler, went back to Jerusalem to quell the rebellion. He took even more captives, including the prophet Ezekiel, and installed Zedekiah as king. Nearly a decade later, Zedekiah rose up against Nebuchadnezzar. In response, King Nebuchadnezzar besieged Jerusalem, eventually destroyed it, and killed King Zedekiah. When the dust settled, the nation of Israel no longer existed. For over a thousand years, from 586 BC until AD 1948, the absence of Israel as a nation bore testimony to the seriousness of turning from God.

How does a nation end up in this shape? How do they go from being divinely blessed to sovereignly destroyed? More importantly, can a nation avoid these same pitfalls today?

THEY REJECTED GOD'S WAYS

> *And he did that which was evil in the sight of the LORD his God, and humbled not himself before Jeremiah the prophet speaking from the mouth of the Lord.*
>
> — 2 CHRONICLES 36:12

Leaders reflect the people they lead. Zedekiah was no different in this regard. As king of Israel, his pride and refusal to humbly submit to God was an indictment against the whole nation. Destruction always comes to those who walk in pride, because God so hates this sin.

Whether from individuals or from nations, He hates pride with a passion!

Pride overestimates itself and underestimates others. Pride places the highest value on its own opinion and completely devalues the opinions of others. The great problem with this sin is that "others" also includes God. Pride was the downfall of Satan. In Isaiah, Satan five times declared, "I will." Pride is about being your own god, pursuing your own will, to get your own way.

At its heart, pride is a spirit of independence and defiance against God. Pride says, "God, I do not completely buy into what you say about things." America is filled with people who are full of pride. They seek to act on their own desires and be their own deity. Egocentric behavior has become the norm in American society. Oh, America have you forgotten that wherever pride travels, destruction is not far behind?

> *For who maketh thee to differ from another? and what hast thou that thou didst not receive? now if thou didst receive it, why dost thou glory, as if thou hadst not received it?*
>
> — 1 CORINTHIANS 4:7

Paul's question to the Corinthians is a powerful one. A thoughtful consideration of his inquiry leads to some questions we ought to ask ourselves. Who gave you the ability to make wealth? Who gave you your position in life? Who allowed you to be born into a family as blessed as yours? The obvious answer to these questions is God! Who are we to get so elevated in our own pride that we believe that we are products of our own making? Without God, we are nothing.

Speaking of Sodom, Ezekiel wrote, "Behold, this was the iniquity of thy sister Sodom, pride, fulness of bread, and abundance of idleness was in her and in her daughters, neither did she strengthen the hand of the poor and needy." Pride precedes turning from God's way, which always brings destruction. What foreshadowed the abominable lifestyle of Sodom was a heart full of pride. What followed its pride was destruction.

THEY REJECTED GOD'S WORDS

and humbled not himself before Jeremiah the prophet speaking from the mouth of the Lord

— -2 CHRONICLES 36:12B

Jeremiah was the prophet who ministered during Zedekiah's reign. Despite being the carrier of God's words, Jeremiah did not find a willing audience in King Zedekiah.

The king refused to listen to Jeremiah's preaching and repent before Jeremiah's God. He was the KING! With a pride-filled heart, Zedekiah determined to do his own thing, even if that meant rejecting the words of God. Seeking to please yourself means displeasing God. Like Zedekiah, you will find that to follow self is to reject God and His ways.

> *And he also rebelled against King Nebuchadnezzar, who had made him swear by God: but he stiffened his neck, and hardened his heart from turning unto the LORD God of Israel.*
>
> — 2 CHRONICLES 36:13

Zedekiah's destruction came as the result of rebellion against King Nebuchadnezzar of Babylon. Yet, this rebellion should have never taken place. Zedekiah had signed a treaty of alliance with Nebuchadnezzar. He had sworn by Jehovah to abide by it, but he broke his promise. Zedekiah had no regard for his promises to man or God because he respected neither. He cared nothing for the righteous wishes of God nor the earthly wishes of man. The only wishes that mattered to Zedekiah were his own.

Rebellion against man and God destroyed Zedekiah. Rebellion is never far from the heart of the prideful. Jeremiah had warned that Zedekiah ought not to rebel against Babylon because they were God's instrument of correction. Zedekiah responded to this warning by beating and imprisoning the prophet, later throwing him into an empty well to be punished.

Although he was Israel's king, Zedekiah's deeds seem more in line with Egypt's pharaoh that had once denied Israel their freedom. Remember Pharaoh's pride-filled heart so bent on his own will that he stubbornly refused to submit to God, even after many plagues of judgment.

Pharaoh said, "Who is the LORD, that I should obey his voice to let Israel go? I know not the LORD, neither will I let Israel go." Like Pharaoh, Zedekiah's pride led him to reject God's Word, a decision that proved costly for both leaders and their nations.

THEY REJECTED GOD'S WARNINGS

> *Moreover all the chief of the priests, and the people, transgressed very much after all the abominations of the heathen; and polluted the house of the LORD which he had hallowed in Jerusalem.*
>
> — 2 CHRONICLES 36:14

I am no plumber, but I am often reminded that many things run downhill. The same is true of organizations and empires. Whatever happens at the top, in leadership, will eventually occur in the people. When leaders are unfaithful, the people they lead will be unfaithful. This pattern is seen clearly in the case of Israel. Rather than positively influencing society, Israel's national and religious leaders were being wrongly influenced by society. Israel polluted the house of the Lord with the worship of Baal, Molech, and Shemosh, the gods of the surrounding heathen nations. Instead of being a light to their neighbors, they adopted the wrong philosophies and practices of their neighbors.

In the New Testament, Jesus refers to believers as salt. Salt is a natural preservative. A barrel of fish would rot unless preserved by the addition of salt. One of the responsibilities of God's children is to hold back decay in the world around us. Sadly, today's church no longer holds a purifying influence on our culture. More often than not, the culture influences the church in its ways. She has become so concerned with political correctness that biblical correctness has been relegated as a philosophy of the past. God and His Word will never conform to worldly standards. He never instructs His messengers to be culturally relevant but prophetically accurate.

On May 18, 1980, Mount St. Helens erupted, killing fifty-seven people. The explosive force, likened to that of a nuclear bomb, was heard six hundred miles away. One would imagine the sound for those near the mountain would have been deafening, but many, rescued within a few miles of the explosion, stated they did not even hear the blast. Scientists explained that the upward thrust of the explosion sent the sound up toward the atmosphere where it bounced back to earth in an outward direction from the mountain. This phenomenon created a "zone of silence," meaning those closest to the eruption missed its roar completely.

I am reminded of Matthew 13 where Jesus, quoting Isaiah, says, "Therefore speak I to them in parables: because they seeing see not, and hearing they hear not, neither do they understand." Many people in Jesus' day were living in a "zone of silence" regarding God's word. A look at America shows many in this generation suffer from the same syndrome.

THEY RECEIVED GOD'S WRATH

> *And the LORD God of their fathers sent to them by his messengers, rising up betimes, and sending; because he had compassion on his people, and on his dwelling place:*
>
> — 2 CHRONICLES 36:15

The word *compassion* used here means "to spare." God

wanted to spare His people from the judgment to come. They brought idols into His sanctuary, yet He loved them. Their sins were not compatible with His righteousness; still, He had a desire to spare them from the punishment of their sin.

God sent messenger after messenger to warn Israel. Time and time again God called them to turn from their wicked ways, but they repeatedly refused. God's compassion for Israel testifies to us of the great patience He continually displays. He is long-suffering to us and "not willing that any should perish." Our world would be wise to learn from the mistakes of Israel, and that God's patience, although great, does come to an end.

> *But they mocked the messengers of God, and despised his words, and misused his prophets, until the wrath of the LORD arose against his people, till there was no remedy.*
>
> — 2 CHRONICLES 36:16

I once heard the relationship between God's wrath and mercy described as a dam holding back water. As people scoff at His prophets and scorn His Word, the waters of God's wrath begin to swell, pressing harder and harder, beating furiously against the dam of His mercy. Even then, God waits. He waits and waits. He doesn't want any to perish. The waters of God's wrath rise and rise until one day, the dam gives way and the wrath of the Lord is released in a torrent that destroys all in its path.

When Solomon dedicated the temple to the Lord, God told Israel,

> "*⁶But if ye shall at all turn from following me, ye or your children, and will not keep my commandments and my statutes which I have set before you, but go and serve other gods, and worship them: ⁷Then will I cut off Israel out of the land which I have given them; and this house, which I have hallowed for my name, will I cast out of my sight; and Israel shall be a proverb and a byword among all people:"*
>
> — 1 KINGS 9:6-7

The fulfillment is found in II Chronicles 36:17-20.

> "*¹⁷Therefore he brought upon them the king of the Chaldees, who slew their young men with the sword in the house of their sanctuary, and had no compassion upon young man or maiden, old man, or him that stooped for age: he gave them all into his hand. ¹⁸And all the vessels of the house of God, great and small, and the treasures of the house of the LORD, and the treasures of the king, and of his princes; all these he brought to Babylon. ¹⁹And they burnt the house of God, and brake down the wall of Jerusalem, and burnt all the palaces thereof with fire, and destroyed all the goodly vessels thereof.*

[20]And them that had escaped from the sword carried he away to Babylon; where they were servants to him and his sons until the reign of the kingdom of Persia:"

There came a time when the dam of God's mercy upon Israel would give way. Nebuchadnezzar invaded the land and destroyed the temple. The costly and sacred items of the temple were carried away to Babylon, and those not taken to Babylon were burned. Jerusalem became a wasteland because they refused to listen to the warnings of God.

America ought to take notice of what happened to Jerusalem. Jerusalem was God's city. There is little doubt that He was more interested in the well-being of Jerusalem than He is in the well-being of America. If God allowed Jerusalem to be destroyed, how likely is He to judge America for the same disobedience, if she refuses to listen to His voice?

> Zedekiah lived out his days without a family, without a country to rule, and without God.

What a tragedy for a nation to walk in disobedience to the point that God's wrath overflows. The tragedy of Israel was worsened because it was completely avoidable. Had Zedekiah led Israel from sin toward God, they would have been spared. However, King Zedekiah was too proud to turn from his own way. As a result, he was taken captive and watched his fellow leaders and his own children be killed. After seeing his children die, Zedekiah's eyes were poked out and he was sent to a prison in Babylon. Due to his rebellion, Zedekiah lived out his days without a family, without a country to rule, and without God.

In 1776 America declared her independence from England. As John Adams signed the declaration of independence, he said, "Whether I live or die, sink or swim, succeed or fail, I stand behind this Declaration of Independence. And if God wills it, I am ready to die in order that this country might experience freedom."[1]

For the next five years, Americans fought for the independence declared in this document. Many of the signers paid the ultimate price for their decision to shake off the monarchy and defy the British Empire. In the end, God gave America the victory. On October 19, 1781, General George Washington accepted the surrender of British General Charles Cornwallis in Yorktown, Virginia.

America soon faced the reality that monarchs and their empires do not take kindly to defeat. Trouble began to brew again in 1812 when British ships started overpowering American merchant ships, often seizing ships, cargo, and sailors. Though newly formed, the United States could not stand for this aggression against its sovereignty, and Congress declared war on Britain. Unfortunately, the war did not go well for America.

By the end of August 1814, the British army occupied the

District of Columbia. Their plan was to capture the main structures in Washington. President Madison and his wife Dolly barely escaped, fleeing the White House just before the British forces reached the capital. It appeared the British would be victorious. Nearly the entire American army were evacuated, killed, or captured. The British moved through Washington with little or no resistance. They commenced burning the city, setting fire to the Capitol Building and the White House. America was falling. Her freedom was aflame!

Suddenly, a tornado, extremely rare in that region, came down the streets of Washington. Trees were uprooted, fences were blown down, and chimneys collapsed. Even the heavy chain bridge across the Potomac River buckled. British cannons were tossed about in the storm. Absolute panic ensued. British soldiers, with no time to take cover, were killed by collapsing buildings and flying debris. The tornado and its effects ended the lives of more British soldiers that night than the American guns killed in the entire War of 1812.

The British Army, shaken by the harsh weather, regrouped near Capitol Hill, and the decision was made to depart Washington that evening. The rain had put out most of the flames before the British Army was even out of sight. Downed trees across the roads hampered their journey. When they finally reached their ships, they discovered two had broken free from their moorings and washed ashore. The storm had devastated their efforts.

As the weather began to return to normal, Sir Alexander Cochrane, the British admiral commented to a local woman, "Great God, Madam, is this the kind of storm to which you are accustomed in this infernal country?"

"No sir," came the reply, "this is a special interposition of Providence to drive our enemies from the city."[2]

The British commander later reported that more of their soldiers were wounded or killed by this catastrophic disaster than from all the firearms the American troops could muster in their defense of Washington. What a testimony to the help of God for a nation who puts Him first! God's hand of favor has remained on America since its beginning. Let us not fail to implore Him for that favor to continue. May we never find ourselves in Zedekiah's position; destroyed because we were too proud to follow God.

A DISASTER DESCRIBED

There were many adventures I anticipated when I earned my driver's license. The freedom and satisfaction of being able to operate an automobile without supervision would surely bring many monumental happenings into my life. However, of all the things I could not wait to experience, an automobile accident was not on my list. Unfortunately, I have had a few of those occurrences in the years since I began driving. Invariably, when an accident occurs, the police are called to the scene. Their investigation of the accident requires the officer to complete a report in which he details the description of the accident.

Recently, my community has experienced a number of thefts. Several residences were burglarized, and many personal belongings were taken. In each situation the homeowner called 911, and a detective was dispatched to investigate the crime scene. Upon examining the scene and speaking with the homeowner, the detective wrote a report that listed the items stolen. The report also included any details of how the burglar gained entry as well as any clues left behind that might lead to his identity. In law enforcement, the story of the accident or crime is documented by the police report.

The first chapter of Isaiah takes me back to those police reports in that it describes the specifics of a tragedy. Isaiah records the results of a nation turning from God toward destruction. The details are not pretty. Like an experienced investigator, Isaiah not only describes the events that transpired but also identifies the contributing factors.

Thousands of years later, as we read his words, we would do well to apply these warnings to our communities and nation. By God's mercy, we are able to avoid their disastrous fate.

Isaiah's account begins with Israel under the reign of a king named Uzziah. During his rule, the nation experienced great prosperity. They enjoyed many contemporary conveniences and extravagances, far more than any of the surrounding countries. They also enjoyed military strength because their borders were successfully defended and even expanded. From a purely human point of view, all was well in the land of Judah. Nevertheless, man's satisfaction does not guarantee God's approval. God had a very different evaluation of Judah. From God's viewpoint all was not well within Judah's borders, and destruction waited just beyond their view.

Judah had, like so many in western Christianity, mistaken prosperity for God's acceptance of their behavior. While they abounded in material wealth, they were poverty-stricken spiritually. The book of Proverbs tells us that "righteousness exalteth a nation, but sin is a reproach to any people." Isaiah's account testifies this fact was true of Judah, but it could also be true of any other nation, including America.

Isaiah, in his burden for his country, seems to be one of a very few that were not reveling in the good times. As Isaiah observed his society, he saw a nation drunken with physical luxury and morally corrupt like no other time in their history. Does this not sound familiar? In the United States, the stock market seems to break daily records, unemployment is at an all-time low, and people are feeling confident in the nation's economy. Yet, there is a great spiritual decline in our country. America desperately needs an Isaiah, a mouthpiece of God, to testify against a people that have forsaken the path of godliness. Indeed, what Isaiah declared about Judah applies to the United States of America. Let us learn from their tragic mistakes so that we can avoid their disastrous fate.

JUDAH FORGOT HER PAST

> *... My people doth not consider.*
>
> — ISAIAH 1:3B

Judah was negligent of both their spiritual upbringing and all that God had done for them. In this verse, the word *consider* means to think rightly or to have an accurate judgment about the current situation. Judah had abandoned righteousness. They had forgotten God's blessings and had forsaken God's commands.

> *Hear, O heavens, and give ear, O earth: For the LORD hath spoken, I have nourished and brought up children,*
>
> — ISAIAH 1:2A

It was God who brought Israel out of Egypt, and it was God who sustained them in the wilderness with food from heaven. It was God who had established them as a nation, and God who blessed them with prosperity. Yet, those who had been blessed so greatly responded like we often do. They attributed their success to their own intellect and ingenuity. Enjoying the richest time in their history, and living under the safe protection of the strongest military, they began to rebel against God and turn from His ways. Since they had reached the top of the proverbial hill, certainly they could maintain the status quo from now on. How wrong they were.

The people did not realize the source of their prosperity was plainly recorded in Scripture. The second book of Chronicles gives the secret of the kingdom's success under Uzziah. "As long as he sought the Lord, God made him to prosper." Judah's prosperity was not their own doing. Rather, it was God who rewarded them for honoring and obeying Him.

America shares that same explanation for her success. Over a century ago, Abraham Lincoln said,

> "We have been recipients of the choicest bounties of Heaven. We have been preserved, these many years, in peace and prosperity. We have grown in numbers, wealth, and power as no other nation has ever grown; but we have forgotten God. We have forgotten the gracious hand which preserved us in peace and multiplied and enriched and strengthened us, and we have vainly imagined, in the deceitfulness of our hearts, that all these blessings were produced by some superior wisdom and virtue of our own. Intoxicated with unbroken success, we have become too self-sufficient to feel the necessity of redeeming

and preserving grace, too proud to pray to the God that made us."[1]

If Lincoln said our nation had forgotten God in his day, what would he say about the spiritual condition of our nation today?

> ...I have nourished and brought up children, And they have rebelled against me.
>
> — ISAIAH 1:2B

It is important that Isaiah's reader understand what rebellion means in this verse. We often think of rebellion as an attitude, but attitudes affect our direction. Here, the word *rebelled* speaks of breaking a covenant or abandonment of a commitment. The relationship between God and Judah was a covenant, and God always honors His word. Yet, like rebellious children, Judah had thrown off her commitment to Him and rebelled.

> The ox knoweth his owner, And the ass his master's crib: But Israel doth not know, My people doth not consider.
>
> — ISAIAH 1:3

"Dumb as an ox" and "bullheaded" are the insults of choice for many seeking to describe anyone with more strength and willpower than mental sharpness. The donkey joins the ox as an animal of choice for insulting the strong-willed and slow-witted. However, Isaiah tells us that even the ox and the donkey are not as foolish as Judah. Even an ox and donkey recognize that they are provided for by their owner. No, donkeys are not bestowed degrees, but these "dumb" animals are smarter than some of God's people because they do not forget where their blessings come from.

Sadly, America joins Judah in the "dumber than a farm animal" category. Just like Judah, the United States has forgotten the true reason for its success and has rebelled against God and His ways. America despises our spiritual heritage and now some publicly declare that those who have a relationship with Jesus Christ are mentally ill.

America, like Judah, was God-centered at her creation. The first community building in our first colony was a church building because our founders wanted a society that was centered on the worship of God. The Puritans first act at Plymouth Rock was to pray and dedicate their colony to God. Roger Williams, a Baptist minister, established Rhode Island. William Penn, a Quaker who established Pennsylvania, was careful to ensure that the governmental policy of the state was that "all treasurers, judges, and elected officials professed faith in Jesus Christ."[2] Penn reasoned that without faith in Christ, an individual could not be deemed worthy to properly govern community affairs.

This idea of the God of Christianity having a central role was not merely a colonial idea. In 1782 the United States Congress passed a resolution that recommended and approved the Bible for use in public schools in order to educate children in morality.[3]

Of course, education in Christianity was taken seriously in the early years of America. The first three universities, Harvard, Yale, and Princeton, were founded to prepare ministers to carry the gospel of Christ to the world. Today these campuses have abandoned those founding principles.

Educational institutions are not alone in having an interest in Christian morality. In fact, the entire legal system of the United States has roots in biblical morality. This fact is not just evidenced in our laws, but on and in the very buildings that represent them. The Supreme Court building, built in 1935, has a carving of Moses and the Ten Commandments. It is sadly ironic that, within this very building, decisions have been made to remove similar monuments from other government structures across the land. The best example of our country rebelling against the God we once honored is spoken by Benjamin Franklin:

> "I have lived, Sir, a long time and the longer I live, the more convincing proofs I see of this truth that God governs in the affairs of men. And if a sparrow cannot fall to the ground without his notice, is it probable that an empire can rise without his aid? We

have been assured, Sir, in the sacred writings that 'except the Lord build they labor in vain that build it.' I firmly believe this; and I also believe that without His concurring aid we shall succeed in this political building no better than the Builders of Babel: We shall be divided by our little partial local interests and partisan projects, and we shall become a reproach to future ages."[4]

These words have lately begun to carry a tragically prophetic ring.

～

JUDAH WAS FOOLISH WITH THE PRESENT

> *Ah sinful nation, a people laden with iniquity, A seed of evildoers, children that are corrupters: They have forsaken the LORD, They have provoked the Holy One of Israel unto anger, They are gone away backward.*
>
> — ISAIAH 1:4

One cannot read this condemnation of Judah and her sin without seeing it is also a condemnation of America and her sin. When a nation can sanction the murder of millions of babies each year, there is little chance that the Holy One of Israel is not angered. When a nation endorses homosexuality, bestiality, and polygamy as acceptable alternatives, that nation has provoked the Holy One of Israel. When a nation forbids prayer to be offered at public gatherings, that nation has enraged the Holy One of Israel. It is apparent that America has rejected God. God's character demands His anger toward those who rebel against Him. There is no avoiding this reality. If God was angry over the sin of Judah, He has to be furious over America's sin.

> *Why should ye be stricken any more? Ye will revolt more and more: The whole head is sick, and the whole heart faint*
>
> — ISAIAH 1:5

The speed at which entire nations change the focus of their attention is astonishing. With the advent of cable news and the internet, our attention spans regarding national events, no matter how tragic, has rapidly decreased. Within a matter of days, the worst of calamities are quickly forgotten, as attention shifts to the newest occurrence. After each tragic event, there is always a chorus of voices saying "we will never forget" and "this must not happen again." Inevitably, the news cycle rolls on, the sun rises and sets and rises again, and we tragically forget.

Perhaps the greatest cause of forgetfulness is prosperity. A boom in the economy erases all worries and fears. As many a coach has stated, "winning fixes everything." No drug can drive negativity from the mind more effectively than abundance. Isaiah's people were no different from us in that regard. Adversity after adversity had plagued them, but their wealth and achievements dulled their awareness. In America's state of prosperity-induced intoxication, we have failed to recognize that these adversities are God's chastisement for our sinfulness.

Despite all the plagues and disasters that came upon them, Judah continued to rebel against God and refused to repent of her evil deeds. In His abundant mercy God asks her, "Haven't you had enough of this judgment and adversity?"

That same question could be asked of America today. Is it possible that the increase in calamities in America is a direct result of our sin? Is God asking us if we have had enough? How much more tragedy, calamity, disaster, and violence? America, have you had enough?

> *From the sole of the foot even unto the head there is no soundness in it; But wounds, and bruises, and putrifying sores: They have not been closed, neither bound up, neither mollified with ointment.*
>
> — ISAIAH 1:6

Isaiah's description of the disaster that unfolded paints the picture of a nation that is beaten, bruised and bloodied from the many consecutive judgments they have suffered.

Judah is described as being a mess of wounds and infection. To make matters worse, they thought their problems were merely a string of unfortunate misfortunes and did not even stop to consider that it could be a result of their wicked ways. They failed to recognize that the pain they experienced was simply sin, doing what sin does. Eventually, sin always harms and leads to destruction, leaving the sinner injured and aching.

One does not have to examine modern-day America very much to see the damage that has been done to our land. A rise in violent crime, earthquakes, tornadoes, hurricanes, wildfires, floods, drought, and record heat waves are plaguing America. Perhaps, these events are all coincidental happenings. Or, could it be, they are the result of a nation rebelling against Jehovah God reaping the consequences of their sins?

> *Your country is desolate, Your cities are burned with fire: Your land, strangers devour it in your presence, And it is desolate, as overthrown by strangers. Except the LORD of hosts had left unto us a very small remnant, We should have been as Sodom, And we should have been like unto Gomorrah.*
>
> — ISAIAH 1:7-9

The terrible condition of Judah would have been worse if not for God's mercy. In fact, it was only by His grace that Judah was not already destroyed like Sodom and Gomorrah. America, too, has avoided destruction so far only by God's great grace and mercy.

JUDAH FAILED REGARDING THE ETERNAL

> *Bring no more vain oblations; incense is an abomination unto me; The new moons and sabbaths, the calling of assemblies, I cannot away with; It is iniquity, even the solemn meeting. Your new moons and your appointed feasts my soul hateth: They are a trouble unto me; I am weary to bear them. And when ye spread forth your hands, I will hide mine eyes from you: Yea, when ye make many prayers, I will not hear: Your hands are full of blood.*
>
> — ISAIAH 1:13-15

With religion comes the danger of ritualism taking the place of true worship of God. Religion often provides a place for people to mask who they are with what they do. Judah was a profoundly religious people, but her outward religious enthusiasm was not accompanied by an inward desire to please God. The people served God with their words, but not with their hearts. The religion of Judah became a ceremony of duty and social norms, but their lack of sincerity displeased God. This wickedness led to the rejection of their worship, sacrifices, services, and even their prayers by God.

What is truly amazing is that God declared their sacrifices repulsive to Him. Did not God command the people to bring sacrifices? Yes, but God desired sacrifices that came from pure hearts full of love for Him. God says, I do not want your sacrifices, for they come from unclean hands and impure hearts.

It was not just the sacrifices that were an affront to God, their Holy Days, New Moons, and Sabbaths had begun to vex Him as well. These rituals were special feast days with ritual productions that were performed throughout the year, much like our Christmas and Thanksgiving services. However, the people had lost sight of the true meaning behind these events, being more concerned with the festivities themselves than the God who gave these celebrations significance. To this tradition God said He was wearied by their holiday services.

Many of our modern day events, programs, and holidays have become just as void of real worship as those in the days of Judah. God is surely wearied of our holidays as well! Sadly, if many pastors told their congregations this message, they would soon find themselves unemployed or preaching to an empty building.

Even the most special rituals of their corporate worship had become vain. The solemn assembly was a specially-called service for prayer and revival. God tells them that even their specially called revival and prayer meetings were worthless. They had become spiritual exhibits to impress others with their righteousness, and all the while they were inwardly living wicked lives before God. God equates church attendance, even the "extra" attendance at revivals and prayer services as sin, if it is done in hypocrisy and with an impure heart.

If their holidays and corporate worship services being spurned by God was not bad enough, God went on to inform them that He was also rejecting their prayers. What an indictment upon the people that their God was refusing to hear their prayers. You will remember that the Psalmist said: "If I regard iniquity in my heart, the Lord will not hear me." That was exactly what Judah had done, and God was turning a deaf ear to their petitions. Every desperate situation they encountered had no audience with their Creator God to ask for His divine assistance.

On the surface, this response seems like God was taking a pretty harsh stance with Judah. However, a closer look at the fifteenth verse reveals that God is responding this way because their hands were full of blood.

Hands full of blood can mean several things from actual violence to improper or pagan sacrifice, to the stain of sinfulness. God could not tolerate their religion because it came from hearts full of rebellion and wickedness.

Please don't miss the point; there is nothing wrong with offering sacrifice, attending worship, or praying in time of need. However, to be effective, these activities must spring from a life that is devoted to God. Religion, from the sacrifices and Holy Days of Judah to the offerings and church attendance of today, must be more than pretense. Unless they come from a sincere heart, they are of no value or meaning at all.

> *This nation's future hinges on the sincerity and holiness of her Christians.*

The vanity of religion is on full display in America. One study of church-attending Americans found that nearly two-thirds said that going to church had no effect on how they lived their daily lives. They were testifying that their religious activities were barren routines, devoid of real encounters with God. They were just going through the motions of worship. Once exiting the doors of the church, they failed to allow their faith to alter their daily conduct. Friends, God is tired of religious events without changed hearts, doctrine that is never put in to practice, and churches full of people claiming to embrace the teachings of the Bible while refusing to live out its teachings in their daily lives. Such a scarcity of sincerity does not bode well for America. This nation's future hinges on the sincerity and holiness of her Christians.

General Douglas MacArthur once said,

"History fails to record a single precedent in which nations subject to moral decay have not passed into political and economic decline. There has been either a spiritual awakening to overcome the moral lapse or a progressive deterioration leading to ultimate national disaster."[5]

Remember, the presence of ten devout people would have spared the city of Sodom from destruction. God always honors a remnant that is true and devout to Him. Perhaps you are a part of a small minority of genuine believers that will save America from destruction.

∼

JUDAH FORSOOK THEIR REPRIEVE

> *Wash you, make you clean; put away the evil of your doings from before mine eyes; cease to do evil; Learn to do well; seek judgment, relieve the oppressed, Judge the fatherless, plead for the widow.*
>
> — ISAIAH 1:16-17

God is a God of justice, righteousness, and holy wrath. He is also a God of mercy, grace, and longsuffering. There are few places this is more evident than in His dealing with

Judah. Right in the middle of His condemnation, God offers them a reprieve. Despite the severity of their rebellion, God extended another opportunity for them to repent and avoid the coming destruction to their land.

This opportunity came in the form of an invitation. God extended an offer to them to move from hypocrisy to honesty. God called them to put their faith into action in their daily lives. This decision meant ceasing all questionable activities, doing good in their homes and communities, and helping those who were in need, especially widows and orphans.

> *Come now, and let us reason together, saith the LORD: Though your sins be as scarlet, they shall be as white as snow; Though they be red like crimson, they shall be as wool.*
>
> — ISAIAH 1:18

Of all the invitations in the Bible, Isaiah records one of the greatest. This verse is often used as a plea for sinners to come to Christ for their personal salvation. Yet, when it was spoken, it was a plea for a nation to repent of her evil ways. The call to reason together is an offer to bring the dispute between God and the nation to an end. It is a plea for Judah to cast herself on the mercy of Almighty God.

> *If ye be willing and obedient, ye shall eat the good of the land:*

> *But if ye refuse and rebel, Ye shall be devoured with the sword: For the mouth of the LORD hath spoken it.*
>
> — ISAIAH 1:19-20

Our God is a covenant-keeping God Who always keeps His word. If there is a breakdown in the relationship between God and man, the responsibility for the breach always lies with man. Thus, it is fitting that God has just spoken of judgment, but now promises to restore Judah to fellowship with Himself if she repented of her evil ways. This lesson is such a simple concept: repent and be blessed, or rebel and be cursed.

Shall we call the roll of extinct empires that have refused to submit to God? We could call the names of Assyria, Babylonia, Persia, and Rome. The list of late, great, global powers that are no more could go on and on. Why is this so? They feared not God, honored not God, and trusted not in God! America's greatest threat comes not from the nations around her, but from God above her. If she continues on her current course, God owes an apology to every nation upon which His sword of punishment has come down.

Nonetheless, we have cause to be encouraged. Even as we look at the description of disaster in Judah and our nation, we must realize there is yet hope for America. Conditions in America are much the same as Judah, but God's operating principles have not changed. The salvation of a nation, or an individual, requires repentance that brings about a submission to God in humility and faith. When these conditions are met, any individual or nation will find God welcoming her back into His fellowship with open arms.

MR. AMOS GOES TO WASHINGTON

I have a fondness for old black and white films. Some modern movies catch my fancy, but there is something special about the motion pictures from earlier years. Before computer animated effects, million-dollar explosions, and risqué scenes became prevalent, filmmakers seemed better at telling stories. Apparently, I am not the only person who enjoys these movies, because there are now entire channels dedicated to reruns of the classics.

Among those old movies and their stars, one actor that has always stood out is Jimmy Stewart. His sincere, relatable demeanor and unique mannerisms made Him one of the most well-loved actors of all time. In 1939, he starred in a movie called *Mr. Smith Goes to Washington,* which was the story of a newly appointed senator from Montana beginning his term in Washington, DC. In the movie, Stewart's character is appalled at the corruption he discovers in the political swamps of his nation. Unwilling to stand for such, and in typical Stewart-character fashion, he boldly confronts the corruption he found, taking much grief along the way for his determination to drain the swamp.

Mr. Smith goes to Washington resonated with audiences and received critical acclaim. Nominated for eleven Academy Awards, it won the prize for "Best Original Story." Noting its significance, the Library of Congress selected the film for preservation in the National Film Registry. Perhaps it was simply good acting and a great script, but it could be the familiar clash of small-town values with big city corruption that resonated with audiences.

The Bible also features such a story. In the book of Amos, we see the account of a country rancher who is called into the big cities of his day to confront their rampant wickedness. Throughout the story, he preaches righteousness and faces opposition for his unpopular positions.

Amos carried a simple yet familiar message to the audiences to which God sent him: repent or expect sudden destruction. Sin is always a dichotomy, leading to one of two outcomes. Either forgiveness is found through genuine repentance, or judgment comes because of continued rebellion. Sin will either be pardoned in Christ or punished in hell. There is no other outcome.

The Old Testament prophets played the role of spiritual

physicians. They diagnosed the spiritual ailments of the people and prescribed God's cure. Sadly, many of the prophets of that time, like many wolves in sheep's clothing today, were more concerned with financial gifts from their audience than the spiritual well-being of their congregation. This vice led them to the perilous pattern of condoning sin.

Amos was a bold preacher who refused to ignore the sin of the people. He was a man of God with a message for the hour. The country preacher confronting the forces of wickedness in his day made for an epic clash made for the silver screen.

THE PREACHER AMOS

> *The words of Amos, who was among the herdmen of Tekoa, which he saw concerning Israel in the days of Uzziah king of Judah, and in the days of Jeroboam the son of Joash king of Israel, two years before the earthquake.*
>
> — AMOS 1:1

If any one ever lived up to their name Amos did. The name *Amos* means burden-bearer or to carry a load and he surely knew what it was to bear the weight of ministering to a sinful people. It is that burden, that weighty knowledge that something must be done, which motivated him to leave his life of obscurity and relative comfort to carry God's message to the people.

Amos hailed from Tekoa, a swampy wasteland located about ten miles southeast of Bethlehem in a wilderness area of Judea. This area was known for its rugged terrain and its rugged people, who were accustomed to the difficulties of living in the outdoors. Amos was a herdsman, one who worked in the breeding and raising of sheep and cattle. According to Amos 7:15, he worked following the flock, not leading like the shepherds, which means he was basically a ranch hand.

Like most agricultural laborers, Amos filled more than one role for his employers. Chapter seven says he was a "gatherer of sycamore fruit." Interestingly, the phrase can be translated to mean "pincher of sycamore fruit." Sycamore trees, which were in abundance in Israel, were plagued by an insect that was detrimental to the fruit's ripening. Thus the "pinchers" squeezed the skin of the fruit to allow the insect to be expelled so the fruit could grow normally. God's plan for Amos was to pinch the places in society to expose the spiritual infestations that hindered the people and their communities.

Then answered Amos, and said to Amaziah, I was no prophet, neither was I a prophet's son; but I was an herdmen, and a gatherer of sycomore fruit: And the LORD took me as I followed the flock, and the LORD said unto me, Go, prophesy unto my people Israel.

— AMOS 7:14-15

In our day, many within the church are more interested in titles and training than a real relationship with God. While formal training is most certainly a necessity in the day in which we live, lineage and learning are no substitute for a man of God who is called and sent by divine decree. In the days of Amos, there were professional prophets who had attended the seminaries of the day, known as schools of the prophets. In addition to attending the schools, many active prophets also came from a family lineage of prophets. Amos makes plain that he was no trained prophet from the schools of ministry, nor was he from a family line of prophetic calling.

Amos was not decrying the idea of education or prophetic lineage. He was addressing the corruption that existed in the religious systems of the day. Many prophets have been corrupted by the wickedness around them. Rather than speaking as the voice of God, they became money-conscious enablers who sought to please the people. Amos' background and message are evidence that was not corrupted by their circles of influence and would minister solely with a concern for pleasing God.

Amos did not seek a ministerial office. He simply did the vocation he knew, working as a farm hand when God called him to prophesy His truth. God had to look beyond all the trained ministers to find a man who would be true to Him was a sad indictment. Obviously, Amos was living a laymen's life that pleased God and we do well to learn from his example. God needs men and women that are true to Him, whatever their occupation.

THE PARISHIONERS OF AMOS

> THE words of Amos, who was among the herdmen of Tekoa, which he saw concerning Israel in the days of Uzziah king of Judah, and in the days of Jeroboam the son of Joash king of Israel, two years before the earthquake.
>
> — AMOS 1:1

THEY WERE RICH.

Understanding the message of Amos requires an understanding of the times and people that he lived amongst. Uzziah was king of Judah for 52 years (767 BC- 739 BC). Jeroboam was king of Israel for 41 years (782 BC- 753 BC). The two kings reigned during a time of unprecedented prosperity and economic growth, with modern conveniences and amenities never before seen. Luxurious homes were in abundance, with many families owning both summer and winter homes.

It was also a time of cultural explosion. Residences were inlaid with fine materials like ivory. The people enjoyed the finest of cuisine and artistic expression, including music. In addition, the people enjoyed their affluence and cultural advantages in relative peace, as their armies went largely unchallenged.

Unfortunately, as is often the case, prosperity led to moral decay for Israel and Judah. It seems often those who accrue wealth begin to rely more on themselves and less on God. This false dependence leads to an indifference toward spiritual matters. One thing can be sure; indifference toward God will never lead to a life that pleases Him. Amos was called to preach to a prosperous people. He soon discovered the rich often make poor listeners.

THEY WERE RELIGIOUS.

When we read of God sending a prophet to preach repentance to the people, we assume they were a crowd unfamiliar with spiritual matters. To the contrary, the people of Amos' day were quite religious, taking pilgrimages to various sacred sites like Gilgal, Bethel, and Beersheba. They flocked to the great religious centers of the day, and attendance at these festivities grew rapidly.

These things sound positive, but remember religious

activity can often be an opiate for a troubled soul. There are many people that use the balm of religion to soothe their convicted conscience while remaining in their sin. Such was the situation in Amos' day. Religion held a place in their lives, but it did not change the way they lived.

Religion without repentance of sin and a relationship with God becomes no more than superstition. The people of Judah and Israel kept many religious customs but were themselves unrighteous. Their religion did little to mask their wickedness.

THEY WERE RUDE.

There was a vast economic divide in Judah and Israel. Alongside the abundance of some, there was severe lack among others. Instead of having compassion for the plight of the poor, the wealthy showed contempt and even ridiculed them in their misery. The rich, consumed with religious ceremony, did not allow their religion to stir their compassion. They had grown indifferent to the needs of their fellow citizens. When Amos saw the opulence of the rich, coupled with apathy toward the poverty around them, he grew angry.

While their religion left them void of compassion, it did nothing to inhibit their carnality. Their superficial, social worship placed no real value on God's commands, leaving them free to make their own rules. To make matters worse, the preachers of the day refused to oppose their wickedness because the rich paid their salaries. It was indeed a dark hour in the lives of God's people.

The putrid morals of the people spread into their leadership. The judges of the day were corrupt and gave out unfair rulings. They dealt dishonestly in order to protect the interests of the wealthy at the expense of the poor.

Into this picture steps Amos, confronting the rottenness of both the religious and governmental powers of the day. His message certainly did not make him a very popular person in society. The people undoubtedly responded much like they do today, wondering who Amos thought he was and how he had the nerve to talk this way.

Dismayed by his message, they were repulsed by Amos' hard preaching. In reality, what they resented the hard truth he preached. Their protest echoes many of today's American churchgoers who want to feel good when they attend church, they prefer their actions and attitudes go unchallenged by the standard of God's Word.

> [12]*Also Amaziah said unto Amos, O thou seer, go, flee thee away into the land of Judah, and there eat bread, and prophesy there:* [13]*But prophesy not again any more at Beth-el: for it is the king's chapel, and it is the king's court.*
>
> — AMOS 7:12–13

The religious establishment of the day would not accept

the truth Amos preached. He simply declared the Word of God, which they neglected, but it was too much for them to bear. Bethel was where the king worshiped. They could not tolerate an uneducated country preacher disrupting the status quo with his hellfire and brimstone messages. Too often, today's church feels like it has outgrown the truth of God's Word. When we worshiped in one-room buildings in the absence of the influential and sophisticated, we welcomed the challenge of hard truth. Now, we have beautiful campuses and our parishioners are among the elite of our communities. Thus we water down God's Word, lest we offend. Any pulpit that does such becomes no better than a doctor who will not tell his patient they have cancer for fear they will disapprove of his message.

THE PREACHING OF AMOS

Sophistication and cultural refinement was absent from Amos' resume. Being a farmhand from Tekoa, he was a rugged outdoorsman, unexposed to the finer elements of society. He was more likely to hot dogs and beans out of Tupperware with a plastic fork than caviar off of fine china with silver. He did not have the most well-tailored wardrobe, but he did have one thing, a calling from God.

For all Amos lacked, he had the assurance of knowing God had called him to deliver a message. What a powerful message it was, but it was not just a message for his day. The message of Amos is a message for America as well. Listen carefully to what the country preacher had to say.

> And he said, The LORD will roar from Zion, And utter his voice from Jerusalem; And the habitations of the shepherds shall mourn, And the top of Carmel shall wither.
>
> — AMOS 1:2

Amos' sermon of the day was an exposition of the third chapter of Joel. Built directly on God's Word, the message spoke from the truth revealed in Scripture. Amos, like every minister today, was tasked with delivering a message from God to his society. The foremost way to fulfill that obligation is to preach Scripture.

Too many ministers waste time with platitudes and pulpit antics. In their attempts to be hip and popular, they preach man's opinion when they should expound upon God's truth revealed in Scripture. The job of the preacher truly is a simple one. He is to relay the message from God to the people that is found in His word. Preachers preaching the Bible are exactly what God wants, and what the nation needs.

"The Lord shall roar out of Zion." Amos's prophecy is just as a lion roars as it leaps upon its prey, God is about to leap in judgment!

"The pastures of the shepherds mourn, and the top of Carmel withers." Mt. Carmel was known for its lush pastures and fertile vegetation. If the top of Carmel was about to wither, it meant total devastation for the rest of the land! God's judgment not only affects the people of a land but also the pastures of that land!

> *Thus saith the LORD; For three transgressions of Damascus, And for four, I will not turn away the punishment thereof; Because they have threshed Gilead with threshing instruments of iron:*
>
> — AMOS 1:3A

The phrase "for three transgressions and for four" occurs eight times in the first two chapters of Amos. Three in this context means full, four means overflowing. So the phrase can be interpreted that God has had all he can take and His judgment is not far away. God's cup of wrath for the people of Israel and Judah are full and overflowing. He will not delay punishment much longer.

Friends, take note that God is overflowing in His wrath toward Israel and Judah, His chosen people. If that is the case, how much more must His wrath be accumulating against America? We as a people are far more wicked than they were. We continue in

> *God has had all he can take and His judgment is not far away.*

our sins while dulling our senses through our religious activities. America must wake up! All our church services, political speeches, and so-called Christian activities do not fool God. Our wickedness abounds, and His wrath is sure to be poured out.

Amos pronounces judgment on seven of Israel's neighbors before addressing their judgment. In total he addresses eight nations, speaking a specific word to each one. However, all of them are relevant to us.

> *Thus saith the* LORD; *For three transgressions of Damascus, And for four, I will not turn away the punishment thereof; Because they have threshed Gilead with threshing instruments of iron: But I will send a fire into the house of Hazael, Which shall devour the palaces of Ben-hadad.*
>
> — AMOS 1:3

First on the list was Damascus, the capital city of Syria. Damascus was sinful in her brutality. Specifically, Amos was addressing the fact that they used implements of farm work, like threshing tools, as weapons to maim and kill people. As creator, God is angered when people deal with cruelness and brutality toward others. He will avenge those wronged.

God says that He will punish the house of Hazeal and Ben-Hadad. Hazael had ruled Syria for 40 years before he was succeeded by his son, Ben-Hadad. Following Amos' prophecy, Damascus was seized in 732 BC, fulfilling God's Word.

> ⁶*Thus saith the* LORD; *For three transgressions of Gaza, And for four, I will not turn away the punishment thereof; Because they carried away captive the whole captivity, To deliver them up to Edom:* ⁷*But I will send a fire on the wall of Gaza, Which shall devour the palaces thereof:* ⁸*And I will cut off the inhabitant from Ashdod, And him that holdeth the sceptre from Ashkelon, And I will turn mine hand against Ekron: And the remnant of the Philistines shall perish, saith the Lord* GOD.
>
> — AMOS 1:6–8

The Philistines, a regular foe of Israel, lived in Gaza, also known as the Gaza Strip, which is west of Jerusalem on the Mediterranean Sea. Though they attacked God's people many times, He was not on a mission of vengeance. Rather a specific sin caused His anger against the Philistines to boil over. Their sin, noted in the phrase "they carry away captive," was slavery.

Slavery was hated by God in past generations in America. He still hates this sin as we traffic young girls for the evil desires of evil men. God brought judgment upon a land for this sin and He will do the same today.

God promised to pour out fire that would devour the

palaces of the Philistines. The defense of any city in that time was its walls. God says that their walls would be destroyed and as the walls burned, so would the palaces. Amos prophesied not even a remnant of the Philistines would remain. True to His word, when God was finished, the Philistines were completely wiped out. In fact, the only thing that remains of them today is the name Philistine.

> [9]Thus saith the LORD; For three transgressions of Tyrus, And for four, I will not turn away the punishment thereof; Because they delivered up the whole captivity to Edom, And remembered not the brotherly covenant: [10]But I will send a fire on the wall of Tyrus, Which shall devour the palaces thereof.
>
> — AMOS 1:9–10

Next on his list was Phoenicia, or modern day Lebanon. Tyrus, a port city, was known for its wickedness. In fact, 1 Kings 16 tells us the king of Phoenicia was father to Jezebel, one of the most wicked people in the Old Testament. They also sinned by supporting slavery.

Again, we see God reacting against cruelty. Here, God's wrath is kindled, and when it is poured out, the buildings, the people, and all their rulers perish. God tells us that vengeance belongs to Him, and when His vengeance comes it is complete.

> [11]Thus saith the LORD; For three transgressions of Edom, And

for four, I will not turn away the punishment thereof; Because he did pursue his brother with the sword, And did cast off all pity, And his anger did tear perpetually, And he kept his wrath for ever: ^{12}*But I will send a fire upon Teman, Which shall devour the palaces of Bozrah.*

— AMOS 1:11–12

The country preacher isn't finished proclaiming the pending judgments of God. Now he speaks of Edom, who as descendants of Esau, were actually distant relatives of Israel and Judah. However, their family ties did not result in good relations with Israel. In fact, Edom dealt in unforgiveness and perpetual hatred toward their kin.

Amos declares that Bozrah, the capital, and Teman, a leading city of Edom, be destroyed for their refusal to forgive their enemies. In 732 BC Tiglah-Pilesar seized Edom, and today all that remains of the nation are the ruins at Petra. Edom, like many other nations in history, discovers that God will not tolerate hatred of His chosen people.

^{13}*Thus saith the* LORD; *For three transgressions of the children of Ammon, And for four, I will not turn away the punishment thereof; Because they have ripped up the women with child of Gilead, That they might enlarge their border:* ^{14}*But I will kindle a fire in the wall of Rabbah, And it shall devour the palaces thereof, With shouting in the day of battle, With a*

> tempest in the day of the whirlwind: *¹⁵And their king shall go into captivity, He and his princes together, saith the* LORD.
>
> — AMOS 1:13–15

The next nation addressed was Ammon. At first glance, they seem like such a savage nation. They would cut open the pregnant women of their enemies and kill the unborn children. Not only did they murder the children of their enemies, they also practiced child sacrifice. As worshipers of Molech, the fire God, they burned their own children alive in the red-hot furnace located in the belly of their idol. What a vicious people!

Yet before we pass judgment, understand that God was angry at them over a sin with which we are quite familiar: abortion. God's anger grew hot because they murdered innocent children, but every day in America we kill thousands of unborn babies. We may not sacrifice babies in the name of Molech, but we discard them like trash in the name of careers, sexual freedom, and women's rights. If God destroyed Ammon over killing innocent children, how can we expect any less?

> *¹Thus saith the* LORD; *For three transgressions of Moab, and for four, I will not turn away the punishment thereof; because he burned the bones of the king of Edom into lime: ²But I will send a fire upon Moab, and it shall devour the palaces of*

> *Kirioth: and Moab shall die with tumult, with shouting, and with the sound of the trumpet:*
>
> — AMOS 2:1–2

When Amos comes to Moab, he addresses a unique situation. First, Moab's sin was they had burned the bones of the King of Edom into lime. Apparently, they had so much hatred for Edom they burned the bones of their king which was symbolic of purging the land of his existence. However, this was a desecration of a corpse, and God was not pleased.

In addition to this unique act, it is also worth noting who the deed was committed against. Moab had not sinned against Israel or Judah, but they had wronged Ammon. Even though God was not happy with the activities of Ammon, He still would not tolerate them being egregiously wronged by another people. Even when God is dealing sternly with a people for their own wickedness, He does not give allowance for others to sin against them.

> [4]*Thus saith the* LORD; *For three transgressions of Judah, And for four, I will not turn away the punishment thereof; Because they have despised the law of the* LORD, *And have not kept his commandments, And their lies caused them to err, After the which their fathers have walked:*

> ⁵*But I will send a fire upon Judah, And it shall devour the palaces of Jerusalem.*
>
> — AMOS 2:4–5

Up to this point, Amos had proclaimed God's anger regarding nations outside Judah and Israel. Now, he brings the focus of his message upon his own people. Judah was guilty of neglecting God's Word and rebelling against His commandments. Instead of making God's Word the center of their lives, they chose to live as they pleased, following the idolatrous ways of their fathers.

> ⁶*Thus saith the LORD; For three transgressions of Israel, And for four, I will not turn away the punishment thereof; Because they sold the righteous for silver, And the poor for a pair of shoes;* ⁷*That pant after the dust of the earth on the head of the poor, And turn aside the way of the meek: And a man and his father will go in unto the same maid, To profane my holy name:* ⁸*And they lay themselves down upon clothes laid to pledge by every altar, And they drink the wine of the condemned in the house of their god.*
>
> — AMOS 2:6-8

Amos has even more to say about Israel than about Judah. It seems that Israel was simply further down the proverbial path away from God. Judah neglected God's Word, and

Israel lived out what that looks like in a nation that continually does so.

The Israelites did not have a societal concern for the poor. Through unjust schemes, predatory economic tactics, and a corrupt court system, the wealthy and powerful were exploiting the poor. The affluent would oppress the destitute with no real fear of justice. The rich simply got richer at the expense of those already in poverty.

A lack of compassion for other people is an indicator of a heart that is turned away from God's leading. Thus, we should not be surprised to find rampant immorality among these hard hearts of Israel. The people were guilty of sexual immorality on a systemic scale. In a normal society, immorality is considered a breach of social construct, and attempts are made to keep it hidden. However, the Israelites practiced immorality openly.

Amos declared the people of Israel not only shamed their own name, but they had shamed the name of God. Jehovah would not stand idly by as they continued in their oppression of the poor, immoral behavior, and drunken revelry. They represented His name, and God cares about His name. The same is true today. If you bear the name of Jesus by calling yourself a Christian, God expects you to bear it well.

> [11]*And I raised up of your sons for prophets, And of your young men for Nazarites. Is it not even thus, O ye children of Israel?*

> saith the LORD. ¹²*But ye gave the Nazarites wine to drink; And commanded the prophets, saying, Prophesy not.*
>
> — AMOS 2:11–12

Notice how Israel dealt with the messengers of God. The prophets were the ones who delivered the message of God to the people. The Nazarites were people who kept themselves pure in service to God. Israel attempted to control the message of the prophets and actively sought to corrupt those who committed themselves to holiness. America is guilty of the same: demanding the pulpits become soapboxes for motivational speakers, and promoting filth through every possible avenue.

> *Behold, I am pressed under you, As a cart is pressed that is full of sheaves.*
>
> — AMOS 2:13

If there is a verse anywhere in this chapter that the modern reader ought to give special attention, it is this one. God describes Himself as a cart that has been overloaded with the sins of the people. He has patiently endured their affronts while they piled on more and more sins. However, this metaphor lends itself to the idea God has reached His capacity. He is going to take no more. Now comes their day of reckoning.

It is unpopular to preach or teach on the wrath of God in the modern American church. We have made God to be a weakling grandfather Who simply endures the grievances of His creation without ever considering discipline. Rest assured this is not the truth. As God views the sins of our nation, He may be patient for a time, but soon He will declare enough is enough. Then comes His day of reckoning.

God sent Amos with a message to deal with eight nations about eight areas of sin. Shamefully, America and the world revel in those same eight sins today. If God judged these nations in the past, He will surely judge us for the same offenses in the present. Our God changes not; He is the same yesterday, today and forever.

- Cruelty to our fellowman - Damascus, Philistia, and Tyre traded slaves for profit. America may have shut down the slave market, but the sin of slavery is revived through the sex trafficking market. Within our own nation, children are exploited, and Americans spend thousands traveling to locations where they indulge themselves in the exploitation of sex slaves. If God judged Damascus, Philistia, and Tyre, He must also judge us.
- Unforgiveness - The Edomites were judged for their bitterness and wrath toward their kinsmen. America seethes with hatred between people

groups. Racism and violence have plagued our nation since its birth. If God judged Edom, He must also judge us.

- Abortion - God will not leave the blood of innocents unavenged. The people of Ammon killed their most helpless members, and God destroyed them. Every day in America, thousands of babies are killed, their bodies dismembered, and the parts sold off or discarded. If God judged Ammon, He must also judge us.
- The rejection of God's Word - Judah turned its back on God's word. Knowing the truth, they turned from it and pursued their own way. This disregard for God led to their destruction. Today, America wants everything from the pulpit except God's Word. Completely abandoning our Christian beginnings, we choose morality based upon public opinion, rather than God's will. If God judged Judah, He must also judge us.
- Immorality - In turning from the holiness of God, Israel became wildly immoral. Despite their righteous beginnings, they were not beyond the judgment of God. God judges immorality, both on an individual and national basis. America has turned from being a God-seeking people to a pleasure-seeking people, pursuing every form of immorality imagined. Fornication, adultery, polyamory, polygamy, homosexuality, gender

confusion, and even pedophilia are becoming commonplace, if not celebrated, in our society. If God judged Israel, He must also judge us.

The specifics of our sinfulness may be different than those of nations to whom Amos preached, but the principles we are violating are the same. God does not change, nor does the morality He expects from His creation. If God dealt grievously with those eight nations, we will not be spared. We cannot avoid the inevitable.

America, destruction is coming.

KATY BAR THE DOOR

Language can be challenging. Words have multiple meanings based on their setting and usage. A word may mean one thing in a literal sense but carry a completely different meaning as an idiom. This duplicity can make for confusing dialogue.

Some common expressions simply make no sense, at least not as we use them. You have probably heard your fair share of these confusing phrases, but have you ever taken the time to think about them? What does it mean when someone is "blowing smoke?" Is it an indicator that they should "put a sock in it?" We really need to "toe the line" on our phrase usage. I could go on and on talking about people being "dressed to the nines" or crying "crocodile tears," but maybe I am "beating a dead horse." These sayings are humorous, but imagine the confusion if someone tried to take them literally. How in the world did they come about? I am sure a study of their origins would be equally informative and entertaining.

One particular saying that echoes from my childhood, whenever my brother and I got into mischief pushing the boundaries of severe discipline, our dad would say, "You boys had better straighten up or it's going to be 'Katy bar the door." I never really knew what the phrase meant, but I sure knew that it was not going to be fun for us should old Katy be forced to barricade the opening of her domicile.

In later years, I learned that the phrase "Katy Bar the Door" was actually a literary reference to a poem written in 1894. It was first put in print in James Whitcomb Riley's *When Lide Married Him*, but is believed to have origins going back to even earlier folk songs and ballads. The phrase basically means that urgent preparations are required for some impending trouble. In the case of my brother and me, the looming doom was our punishment, and Katy served as our reminder to take note and change our behavior.

The third chapter of Amos carries a "Katy bar the door" message. In this chapter, the prophet warns Israel that God's judgment is coming and they had better brace for the impact. Of course, no amount of readiness can weather the storm of God's anger. Israel's only chance of avoiding destruction was to turn from their wicked ways and wholeheartedly return to following Jehovah.

Just as my brother and I often struggled with changing our

behavior in response to dad's warning, Israel had to wrestle with the message that Amos preached. If they would repent and submit to God, they would be spared. But, to reject the message and continue in their sin, meant Katy bar the door.

THE RELATIONSHIP IN JUDGMENT

Hear this word that the LORD hath spoken against you ...

— AMOS 3:1A

Like many ministers, Amos knew that his audience did not always listen to his sermons, so he begins by telling them to take special notice because his message was of utmost importance. This is not the only time God's Word demands full attention. In Revelation chapters two and three, hearing is called for seven times while Romans tells us that "faith cometh by hearing."

Adequate and engaged hearing is vital to receiving a message from God. Many times we hear His words but fail to grasp their meaning. Amos knew flippancy from this audience was likely. He had concern that his hearers would not receive the message, yet he knew that this message from God must not be taken lightly. Amos came with a serious warning that carried serious consequences. Israel was not the only audience from which God expected a sober response, this passage contains a message for us today. Take heed.

> *Hear this word that the* LORD *hath spoken against you, O children of Israel, Against the whole family which I brought up from the land of Egypt, saying,*
>
> — AMOS 3:1

The message of Amos begins with a reminder regarding the very existence of Israel. Their creation and survival as a nation was an act of God's grace. Their exodus from Egypt, wilderness journey, and early years of the kingdom were ordained and orchestrated by God Almighty. Israel's history is full of God's miraculous provision and divine intervention. Israel would be little more than a footnote in history were it not for the unmerited favor of Jehovah God.

> *For thou art an holy people unto the* LORD *thy God: the* LORD *thy God hath chosen thee to be a special people unto himself,*
>
> — DEUTERONOMY 7:6

Israel reaped the benefits of a special position in God's sight. Since Abraham, Isaac, and Jacob, they had enjoyed a special relationship with God as His chosen people. Yet, they were not chosen because they were special; they were special because they were chosen. There was nothing about Israel that made them worthy of God's kindness, but He chose them to be His out of His great love and compassion.

Bestowing grace and blessing upon the undeserving is the foremost characteristic of our God. God does not smile upon people because of their strength or capability, but because of His strength of character. God does not prefer the most prominent and powerful in society, but He reaches for the least and waits patiently for the last of society.

Israel was blessed to be the focus of His kind affections. As a believer, you too are a recipient of His divine grace and favor. How blessed you are to be a chosen one of God!

> *According as he hath chosen us in him before the foundation of the world, that we should be holy and without blame before him in love:*
>
> — EPHESIANS 1:4

We all have childhood memories that stand out more than others. For me, one of those fond recollections is the first time I was chosen to receive a reward. It happened as part of a candy fundraiser my school held when I was in the fifth grade. Each box sold placed your name in a drawing to participate in the "jump for dollars" where contestants could win cash based on their leaping ability. When the time of drawing came, I was astonished to hear my name called. Of all the students that could have been summoned, I could not believe it was me! Although it is a quaint memory, I still fondly recall how it felt to be chosen to receive a blessing.

In a way, I still get that feeling when I think about God choosing me. What a thought! Our Heavenly Father has chosen us! He chose us to be blessed with the eternal riches of Christ. He appoints us with favor to live in blessing and accomplishment far beyond our own strength. What a blessing it is to be chosen!

> *You only have I known of all the families of the earth: Therefore I will punish you for all your iniquities.*
>
> *— AMOS 3:2*

Privileged position often brings pride. Israel was so haughty regarding their selection by God it became a stumbling block to them. Much like American Christians like to point out our nation's Christian heritage, Israel was quick to acknowledge their position before their pagan neighbors. Unfortunately, they became presumptuous in their relationship with God and forgot the truth that with great position comes great responsibility.

As a child, I got my fair share of discipline from my father. Sometimes I got in trouble for things that I had been involved in with kids who lived nearby. Even though they shared the guilt, my father never once disciplined any of the others. They were not his children. His great concern was about my behavior, not theirs. A father disciplines His own children.

When Abraham accepted God's promise by faith, he became part of God's family. The two entered into a covenant relationship, uniting in a "cutting covenant" ceremony. This connection meant that Abraham's bloodline, Israel, were God's children. As God's children, they were rightful recipients of God's divine discipline.

God had delivered Israel out of slavery and made them a nation, because of His covenant with them. This covenant union meant God and Israel had a family-like relationship. Amos brings a message to remind them since God had chosen them as His own, He expected more out of them than He did the pagan nations around them. God is also letting them know, as His children, they should expect Him to apply discipline when they wander in a forbidden direction.

With family relationship comes the necessity to live worthy of the family name. When Amos arrives on the scene in Israel, they had drifted far from their familial responsibilities. God sent Amos to proclaim His judgment and discipline were coming. This pending judgment was not simply because they had been sinful, but because they had violated their covenant and had dishonored the name of their heavenly Father.

Every believer is in a covenant familial relationship with God. What a beautiful picture of grace! God makes us, unworthy as we are, His own children. Yet being God's child means, when we rebel, we are the first in line for His chastening. Hebrews 12 tells us that God applies discipline to those He loves and will sometimes use pain to correct them. Chastening is not God rejecting His child, but rather his means for drawing them into a closer relationship with Him.

THE REASON FOR JUDGMENT

God is not a tyrant. He desires for us to understand His justice; otherwise, His mercy and grace is pointless. Amos does not just proclaim imminent punishment, he lays out five examples to help them understand God's reasoning. Reading them, we see clearly that God is justified in punishing Israel. Also notable is how similar their offenses are to our offenses. If God was justified in punishing Israel, He is more than just in chastening America.

Can two walk together, except they be agreed?

— AMOS 3:3

Few of us would pick hitchhiking as our primary mode of transportation. Outside of a dire emergency, most of us would never want to put ourselves in a vehicle with a potentially dangerous stranger. In the same way, in Amos' day, you would not join with a stranger to make a journey or to walk through the wilderness. They could have impure motives and perhaps even accomplices lying in wait to rob you of your possessions or your life. Thus, no one wanted to journey with someone with whom they were not acquainted.

Sometimes people begin in agreement, but then the dynamic changes. Imagine yourself sitting in a shopping mall engaging in one of life's most entertaining activities: people-watching. You see a young man and woman walking close together, sometimes holding hands, and sometimes leaning against one another. You can almost see the sparks of romance. Suddenly their romantic stroll screeches to a halt. You see them face one another in a heated discussion, then part and walk, scowling, in opposite directions. What happened? They fell out of agreement with one another, and their journey together ended.

Amos is making the point that you cannot walk with God if you are not in agreement with Him. If you are not going in the same direction, how can you walk together? At one point, Israel had walked in agreement with God, but they turned from His ways. Amos wants them to understand their choices have consequences. They could not choose to live opposite of God's desire and still be in fellowship with Him. They desperately needed to correct their course.

The same may be true of you. Many times we claim to be followers of God, yet our actions and thoughts are completely contrary to Him. It is important to weigh each decision according to the Will and Word of God.

Are you walking with God? Do you agree with Him? Do you agree with His Word about sin? What about repentance? Do you agree with God about marriage, child-rearing, finances, the local church, and morality? If you are not in agreement with God, you are not walking with Him!

> *Will a lion roar in the forest, when he hath no prey? Will a young lion cry out of his den, if he have taken nothing?*
>
> — AMOS 3:4

The second example used by Amos is the lion. A lion does not roar when it is in the act of a hunt, because the prey, being alerted by the roar, would run to safety. The roar of the lion will only be heard after the kill, an announcement of victory and a call for the other lions of the pride to join the feast. The roar comes only after the conquest.

God's judgment operates on the same principle. Like the roar of the lion, it does not come immediately. When does it come? The answer is plainly shown again and again in Scripture. God's judgment comes when His children have not lived in obedience and respect of His Word. Friends, for America, the time for judgment is overdue.

> *Can a bird fall in a snare upon the earth, where no gin is for him? Shall one take up a snare from the earth, and have taken nothing at all?*
>
> — AMOS 3:5

Trapping an animal requires patience and planning. A bird could only be trapped when someone has gone to the effort of setting a trap. Additionally, the trapper will only be successful if they have been strategic in the setting. In the bird hunter's trap, we see another great example of God's dealing in discipline. God does not just pour out wrath because He has nothing better to do. Much like the trapping of a bird follows willful action; God's judgment only comes as a result of the willful disobedience of His children.

> *Shall a trumpet be blown in the city, and the people not be afraid?*
>
> — AMOS 3:6A

Today's trumpets are used to make music, but in the time of Amos, they were not mere instruments of song. Biblical trumpets were more like sirens used to warn of impending danger. Not long ago, panic hit Hawaii as someone pressed the wrong buttons, setting off the missile warning systems on the island. In a moment, what was intended as a simple drill became disastrous. People panicked because those alarms do not sound without a confirmed and justified reason.

Amos connects the idea of the warning system before God's wrath. Neither one occurs without a reason. No one would expect the warning system of today or the trumpet of Amos' day to be sounded unless danger was truly imminent. Crying wolf is not God's method. His judgment only comes when its arrival is necessary and justified.

> ...shall there be evil in a city, and the LORD hath not done it?
>
> — AMOS 3:6B

The last of the examples Amos uses is perhaps the most alarming. In this statement, Amos makes clear these troubles and disasters come upon Israel had been sent by God. Israel had dishonored Jehovah, and He was personally judging them for their actions.

Not every disaster that comes upon our world is an act of punishment by God, but we would be foolish to believe that none are the work of divine discipline. Amos instructed them from the position God is sovereign over the universe. There is a heavenly plan to bring glory to God through every situation and circumstance.

As bad as our troubles are, we are remiss to only view trouble as detrimental. Every disaster brings an opportunity. In difficulty, we should find an opportunity to examine ourselves for disobedience. If we find that we have not been walking in agreement with God, then repentance is in order. This discipline is where Israel failed. They did not practice self-examination. They did not depart from their wicked ways, and destruction was the result of their continued rebellion.

> *Surely the Lord God will do nothing, But he revealeth his secret unto his servants the prophets.*
>
> — AMOS 3:7

Again, we see God going beyond what is deserved. The people did not deserve a warning, and they most certainly did not deserve an opportunity to repent of their rebellion. Yet in patience and mercy, God sends Amos to warn them to repent and be spared of His chastening. What mercy!

God is so longsuffering even when His wrath must be poured out, He is not willing that any should perish. God will not destroy a people before he sends a warning. But,

His warnings are not empty threats. As individuals, and as a nation, we should be careful to respond when God speaks to us about our wrongdoing.

> *The lion hath roared, who will not fear? The Lord GOD hath spoken, who can but prophesy?*
>
> — AMOS 3:8

The prophets were God's warning system to His people. Just as He sent messengers in that day, He is sending messengers in our day. God is raising up modern-day prophets, to stand and rebuke the wickedness of society and the church. Unfortunately, this message of God's wrath is often scorned in the modern church. Just like Israel, we often fail to see what a blessing an Amos is.

America, you are being warned. Destruction is coming if you do not repent. Thank God for His warning and for his messenger who boldly carries it to the people.

THE REPROACH OF JUDGMENT

> *Publish in the palaces at Ashdod, And in the palaces in the land of Egypt, And say, Assemble yourselves upon the mountains of*

> Samaria, And behold the great tumults in the midst thereof, And the oppressed in the midst thereof.
>
> — AMOS 3:9

How many times have you witnessed the shameful spectacle of some CEO, politician, or community leader being led into a police station in handcuffs? How many times have we seen video clips of a tearful minister addressing their congregation after a moral failure? These are not scenes of joy. They are stark displays of shame as the world looks on.

There is a disgraceful scene like this in the story of Israel. God assembles the Egyptians and Philistines on the mountains of Samaria to witness Israel's failure. How embarrassing it was for Israel, God's chosen, to be mocked and ridiculed by their neighbors. Shame is not exclusive to Israel. Rebellion against God's Word, if continued, will always end in public dishonor.

> For they know not to do right, saith the LORD, Who store up violence and robbery in their palaces.
>
> — AMOS 3:10

Israel was far from the days of following God's daily leading in the wilderness. Having continued so long in sin, the conscience of the people was dulled. They no longer had the ability to discern between right and wrong, so they ended up in a world of relativism where good was called evil and evil was called good.

America is in the same predicament. We promote promiscuity and perversion but ridicule abstinence as prudish. We honor the reprobate and condemn the virtuous. It is a dark day when a society has lost its moral compass. Sadly, that is exactly where America finds itself.

> *Therefore thus saith the Lord God; An adversary there shall be even round about the land; And he shall bring down thy strength from thee, And thy palaces shall be spoiled.*
>
> — AMOS 3:11

Our great God is longsuffering. Although He will send judgment and chastening, He does not desire that anyone would have to feel His wrath. Even as His justice calls for our punishment, His love calls for our forgiveness. This truth is made evident in how consistently God sends warnings before punishment. He sends thunder before lightning, but it is up to us to take shelter in His grace.

Thus saith the LORD; As the shepherd taketh out of the mouth of the lion two legs, or a piece of an ear; So shall the children of Israel be taken out that dwell in Samaria in the corner of a bed, and in Damascus in a couch.

— AMOS 3:12

Shepherds, by necessity, must be vigilant and protective of the animals in their care. In the time of Amos, if a shepherd lost an animal, he was required to pay for it. The only exception was if he could prove some wild beast killed it. The only way to prove such an attack had occurred was to bring back any pieces of the animal he could find.

This gory evidence was the proof that the livestock was killed by some animal rather than being lost by some incompetent shepherd. Perhaps, the most famous occurrence of this idea in the Bible occurs in the story of Joseph. By dipping his distinctive coat into blood, Joseph's brothers used this principle to trick their father into believing a wild animal had devoured him.

To get his point across, Amos uses this graphic idea of an animal ripped to death by a lion. The prophet gravely warns that Israel is heading for destruction. They are going to be torn to pieces, utterly destroyed, because of their wickedness and rebellion.

[13]Hear ye, and testify in the house of Jacob, saith the Lord GOD,

> *the God of hosts, ¹⁴That in the day that I shall visit the transgressions of Israel upon him I will also visit the altars of Beth-el: And the horns of the altar shall be cut off, And fall to the ground.*
>
> — AMOS 3:13–14

The horns of the altar were a place that symbolized grace. In the Old Testament, a person who was guilty of a crime could find mercy by going to the temple and grabbing the horns of the altar. In a New Testament context, they are a foreshadow of the wrath of God being restrained by the sacrifice of Jesus.

Now we see the significance of Amos' words. He prophesies there would be no horns on the altar for a person to seize. God is letting them know a time will come where no mercy is found, only wrath and judgment. Israel is being warned to repent while it is possible. This warning is the same for us as it was for them. We must repent while mercy can be found.

America's sin cannot go unjudged. God is merciful to send messenger after messenger. Again and again, we have heard their warnings of wrath to come. Yet, again and again, we fail to heed the words of warning. How long will God be patient? How long will He continue to deal in kindness while we mock Him and His Word? Are there any horns on the altar for us?

ME, MYSELF, AND I

The corporate world often wastes time chasing problems and solving symptoms without getting to the source of the problems. Hours are spent "putting out fires" while the arsonist continues his work undisturbed. To combat this foolishness, organizations use something called a "root cause analysis" to systematically identify where processes are breaking down. Issues can only be solved permanently by attacking the root cause.

What would a root cause analysis of modern-day American Christianity reveal? What is our greatest problem? Some would say a lack of faithfulness; others may point to wrong priorities, while others might speak of sexual immorality and ethical misconduct. While all of these are legitimate issues, they are merely the fruits of the actual "root cause" that must be fixed.

I believe the greatest problem in American Christianity is an incorrect view of God. It perhaps seems an unlikely culprit, but one's view of God is the foundation upon which all attitudes and actions evolve. Our theology, knowledge, and understanding of God directly impact our daily lives.

One of my friends in college constantly struggled with getting involved with things he knew were wrong for him. You could talk to him until you were blue in the face, but his actions never changed. More confusing was the fact that he would quickly agree with each critic's analysis of his ungodly behavior. Yet, despite his acknowledgment of God's displeasure, his actions never changed.

Like any series of wrong choices, the consequences of his sins began to pile up. Eventually, he was taken into custody. He nearly destroyed his marriage and family. Finally, he changed. This about face was no small change, but a radical transformation that affected every area of his life. He went from performance to passion in his faith. He memorized Scripture and never missed church or Bible study. He stopped coasting spiritually and became the spiritual leader of his home with a passion for Jesus.

"What happened to you?" I asked one day as we played golf. "You have radically changed spiritually, and you're totally different. What happened?"

I will never forget his reply. "What changed in my life was

my view of God. I realized that I am not the king of the universe, but God is. Since He is the true king, I should be his devoted servant. As long as I live on this planet, I want to be a servant of God, and I want Him to rule my life."

This enlightenment is what the American church needs. They need a drastic change in their view of God. When your view of God changes, it changes everything in your life. This revelation takes people from being uncommitted stragglers to devoted followers, serving God with no reserve.

The Bible is full of stories of people whose view of God was faulty. One of the most notable is Jonah. Jonah attempted to live as if he was his own god and could make his own choices without repercussions. His self-focused mentality is rampant among American Christians. Sadly, Jonah endured terrible consequences as a result of his wrong thinking. Perhaps, a closer look at his life will encourage us to correct our own self-focused vision.

JONAH HAD A DISRESPECT FOR GOD'S WORD

> *Now the word of the LORD came unto Jonah the son of Amittai, saying,*
>
> — JONAH 1:1

There is no greater honor than God speaking to you. Jonah received clear instructions directly from God. This guidance was not the suggestion of an influential man, but the Word of the All-Powerful God of the Universe. What a humbling honor! What an incredible responsibility! The authority behind this clear command was God Himself. Yet, despite the honor and supremacy, Jonah did not reverence nor submit to this Word from Almighty God. Instead, he rebelled and did the opposite.

Upon reading the story, it is easy to ridicule Jonah for his choices. However, many times we do likewise and reject the Word of God in our lives. We receive the Word of God in our own personal copy of the Bible, but too often we reject it. Even though we display it in our homes and wear it on our shirts and bumper stickers, our actions reject God's Word. We reject it when we say it is old-fashioned. We reject it when we place worldly wisdom above heavenly wisdom. We reject it when we prioritize every other activity, but neglect our time in the Bible. Friends, we are dealing with a crisis in our land: the neglect of God's Word.

Arise, go to Nineveh...

— JONAH 1:2

Although God's Word to Jonah was brief and direct, it was

clear and understandable. The word translated *arise* indicates an action of haste and urgency. The word translated *go* was a military command used to direct troops to head to battle and engage the enemy. This directive was an absolute order to be carried out with urgency, but Jonah disregarded this clear command, deeming it unimportant.

How brazen is one to ignore a command from the God of the universe? However, be careful not to point the finger at Jonah. Everyone with access to a Bible has received a clear, direct Word from God to love Him with all our heart, soul, and mind. It is a specific word, a straightforward word, but too many times, we love the things of the world more than the things of God. Too often, like Jonah, we disregard His Word.

> *Arise, go to Nineveh, that great city...*
>
> — JONAH 1:2

When Jonah received his command from God, he was 500 miles from Nineveh, but he heard of their deplorable ways. Jewish people hated the Ninevites. Their hatred was not without cause, because Nineveh was known to be the home of an exceptionally cruel and brutal people. The Ninevites were known to torture their enemies with agonizing punishment. They were so brutal that their evil deeds stood out as the most inhumane of their pagan neighbors.

Knowing how wicked Nineveh was, why would God call it a "great city". Here, *great* does not indicate any sort of moral goodness. Rather, it speaks of the strength of the city. Nineveh was said to be 60 miles wide, with a population of over one million people. Famous for its architecture, Nineveh boasted the most unique and beautiful structures in the known world of their day. Over 16,000 tablets of learning were compiled in Nineveh, a testament to their academic prowess. Despite its list of amazing features, Nineveh was most famous for its atrocities. The city's people were known as the most wicked, perverted, and cruel people on earth.

> *Arise, go to Nineveh, that great city, and cry against it; for their wickedness is come up before me.*
>
> — JONAH 1:2

God had a very specific purpose in mind for sending Jonah to Nineveh. He wanted him to "cry against" the city. The phrase *cry against* means to declare opposition to someone or something in a passionate way. To the modern reader, the word *cry* lends itself to the idea of physical tears, which we very well could include. However, the primary interpretation is a bold declaration against the sins of the city. Going to a city that was an enemy of his homeland, not to mention famous for cruelty, would be a frightening assignment for Jonah. What would the people think of him and his actions? How would Nineveh respond to his message?

Fear is a debilitating force, even when it comes to obeying the commands of God. How often does the fear of man control our decisions? Do you ever weigh the opinions of man more important than the opinion of God? Like Jonah, every believer has a word from God to go into the world and declare the love and redemption of an all-powerful God. How are you responding to that word?

The Council of Constance tried John Huss in January of 1415. Arrested and charged with forty counts of blasphemy, Huss was mocked and derided by the council members. They were so enraged at his words, they condemned him to burn at the stake. The council ordered the crown of his head cut off using a pair of garden shears. Afterward, they painted demons on a paper bishop's hat and placed it on his head. The words "A Ringleader of Heretics" was boldly written across the hat.

Huss was then led to a metal stake where he was chained. Bundles of his books were placed around him, stacked to his neck. There, on his forty-second birthday, he was asked to recant his teachings. He replied, "What I have taught with my lips, I now seal with my blood."[1] As the flames rose around him, he sang a hymn with such fervor that it could be heard over the roar of the flames and the noise of the crowd. His remains joined John Wycliffe's at the bottom of the Rhine River. Huss valued God's word so highly he willingly gave his life for it. The testimony of John Huss demands an answer to the question, "How much do you value the Word of Almighty God?"

JONAH HAD A DISDAIN FOR GOD'S PRESENCE

> *But Jonah rose up to flee unto Tarshish from the presence of the LORD, and went down to Joppa; and he found a ship going to Tarshish: so he paid the fare thereof, and went down into it, to go with them unto Tarshish from the presence of the LORD.*
>
> — JONAH 1:3

After receiving the Word from Almighty God, Jonah went in the opposite direction God sent him. There was no effort to fulfill God's command at all. Rather, he utterly rebelled and sailed in the opposite direction.

There is a very disturbing phrase in this verse. It says he went to Tarshish "from the presence of the Lord." Leaving the presence of God meant he forfeited the blessing and power of God upon his life. When a person leaves God's abiding presence, they also lose His anointing presence. Jonah withdrew himself from God's direction. Therefore God withdrew His hand of blessing upon Jonah. Why anyone is willing to forfeit the guiding and providing hand of God upon their life is incomprehensible, but many continue to make that foolish choice today.

It is said, "there are only two roads in the Christian life: one leads to Tarshish, and one leads to Nineveh. One path takes us to the will of God and one takes us from the will of God." Be forewarned: when you run from God's will, you head toward a place of heartache and loss. In the story of the prodigal son in Luke 15, a young man with grand plans and big dreams made the terrible choice to walk away from his father. That choice led to a life of grief and utter disappointment. Lamentably, that result is always the case when someone runs from the will of God.

Along with a root cause analysis, organizations find a cost analysis worthwhile when making changes. The cost analysis on Jonah's trip to Tarshish reveals the disastrous expense of his foolish choice. It cost him the time that he could have used for the Lord. It cost him money to finance the trip, not to mention his belongings that were thrown overboard. He lost his testimony with those who had observed him. Worst of all, he lost the most valuable gift he possessed, the hand of God on his life.

JONAH HAD A DISBELIEF IN GOD'S POWER

But the Lord...

— JONAH 1:4

Details determine the success or failure of any undertaking. In fact, one small detail can turn a perfectly planned project upside down. Despite all of Jonah's planning and calculations, he forgot one colossal detail -- God Almighty! The journey began with smooth sailing toward Tarshish, but his wrong choice affected his world. It instantly flipped upon its axis, and all those close to him felt the consequences of his choices.

But the LORD sent out a great wind into the sea...

— JONAH 1:4

The word translated *sent* is a Hebrew word that means to hurl or launch. That definition means God initiated and directed a storm just for Jonah. This decision was no coincidence. God designed a storm to correct His disobedient servant. Do not be surprised if you disobey God, if He designs a storm to draw you back to Himself. The Bible clearly teaches God corrects every son in whom He delights. This reality should inspire us to consider our choices carefully regarding our obedience to God.

Jonah provides a valuable lesson for all who heed it. Refusing to obey the Word of God and rebelling against His will is the path to sorrow.

> God corrects every son in whom He delights.

God always sends a storm into the life of a rebellious child. In the words of Stuart Briscoe, "God is ready to move heaven and earth to get His message through to those who turn their back on Him!"[2]

> *But the LORD sent out a great wind into the sea, and there was a mighty tempest in the sea, so that the ship was like to be broken*
>
> — JONAH 1:4

Choices have consequences. Yet many struggle to apply its truth to their decision-making process. The Scripture teaches we reap what we sow. Whether good or bad, our choices always have consequences. The storm, in which Jonah found himself, along with the unfortunate souls on the boat with him, was a direct result of his rebellion against the Word of God.

> *Then the mariners were afraid, and cried every man unto his god, and cast forth the wares that were in the ship into the sea,*

to lighten it of them. But Jonah was gone down into the sides of the ship; and he lay, and was fast asleep.

— JONAH 1:5

For the average person, it does not take a large storm to make us afraid. However, the experienced sailors in this story had seen their share of storms. This storm God sent was so violent it caused even these skillful sailors to be shaken by its deadly force.

In stark contrast to the deep concern of the crew is the callousness of Jonah. The sailors fell to the ground and cried out to their gods, but Jonah was so rebellious not only did he not petition God, he was asleep!

One summer I came home from college and sought work through an employment agency. They sent me to the worst job of my life. I spent eight hours a day standing beside a conveyor belt putting lids on countless cans of contact solution as they passed in front of me. It was not glamorous, nor was it enjoyable, and I certainly have not bragged about it on any resume. After several weeks of this endlessly monotonous work, my hands were so calloused that a sharp pinprick to my hand felt no sensation. The same is true when a Christian continues to rebel against the Holy Spirit. The more they rebel, the more calloused they become until they no longer feel His leading or conviction in their life.

The presumptuous attitude of man knows no limit. Every character in this story was submissive to God. The sea, the storm, the fish, the lots, and the sailors all obeyed God. The solitary player in the entire narrative that refused God's command was Jonah. What a sad indictment to man's rebellious nature. Before judging Jonah too harshly, however, you should ask yourself, "Am I submissive to God? Am I willing to do His Will and His work, whenever and whatever He asks of me?"

> *So the shipmaster came to him, and said unto him, What meanest thou, O sleeper? arise, call upon thy God, if so be that God will think upon us, that we perish not.*
>
> — JONAH 1:6

Jonah was awakened from his sleep by the captain of the ship who urged him to pray to his God for deliverance. Here we see another stark contrast. Jonah, the prophet of Jehovah, has less spirituality than the pagan sailors who were quick to turn their thinking to their superstitions and false deities. While the crew members individually wondered if their actions were the cause of the storm, Jonah's silence showed his lack of respect for God's opinion of his actions. His silence also revealed a lack of concern for those whom his actions affected. This reaction too, is a symptom of a rebellious heart which increases in hardness toward not just God, but other people as well.

> *⁷And they said everyone to his fellow, Come, and let us cast lots, that we may know for whose cause this evil is upon us. So they cast lots, and the lot fell upon Jonah. ⁸Then said they unto him, Tell us, we pray thee, for whose cause this evil is upon us; What is thine occupation? and whence comest thou? what is thy country? and of what people art thou?*
>
> — JONAH 1:7-8

Our Sovereign God works through the most bizarre of circumstances to accomplish His will. In this story, He controls the roll of dice to bring His rebellious servant to justice. When the dice completed their roll, and Jonah was exposed, the sailors interrogated him about his role in this violent storm. It was an embarrassment for Jonah to admit to these pagan sailors they were in the storm because of his rebellion against Jehovah God.

> *⁹And he said unto them, I am an Hebrew; and I fear the LORD, the God of heaven, which hath made the sea and the dry land. ¹⁰Then were the men exceedingly afraid, and said unto him, Why hast thou done this? For the men knew that he fled from the presence of the LORD, because he had told them.*
>
> — JONAH 1:9-10

Again we see the stark contrast between the supposed child of God and the pagan sailors around him. These sailors showed more respect for Jehovah than Jonah, God's own prophet. How awkward it was for Jonah to explain that he was a messenger of God to the sailors whose lives his rebellion had endangered. Still, it was no more awkward than for a modern-day "Christian" to explain they serve God while their lifestyle screams the opposite.

The story is told of a soldier from the army of Alexander the Great. In the heat of battle this despicable soldier abandoned his comrades and fled from the fight. When he was captured, he was brought before Alexander the Great. The soldier begged for mercy and promised his allegiance would be unfailing if only he were to be granted another opportunity to serve. The great conqueror obliged, but, as the soldier was leaving, the emperor asked his name. The soldier turned and dropping his head stated his name: Alexander. The ruler seethed with ire and shouted for the soldier to change his name or else change the way he was living. What a word for us today, not as soldiers, but as Christians. Far too many Christians claim to be followers of Christ but have lives that are not representative of His name.

> ¹¹*Then said they unto him, What shall we do unto thee, that the sea may be calm unto us? for the sea wrought, and was tempestuous.* ¹²*And he said unto them, Take me up, and cast me forth into the sea; so shall the sea be calm unto you: for I know that for my sake this great tempest is upon you.*
>
> — JONAH 1:11-12

At the beginning of this chapter, the concept of a "root cause analysis" was introduced. Here Jonah does his own analysis of the situation, but he fails to include one very important factor -- repentance. Throughout the Bible, God demonstrates extravagant mercy upon the wicked who repent of their evildoing. It seems that the hardness of his heart toward Nineveh prevented Jonah from expressing true repentance. He took the blame for causing the storm, but he declined to confess and forsake his sin before God. Perhaps, Jonah realized that repentance would include doing God's will and preaching to his enemies, the people of Nineveh. Many people today live in rebellion because they know what God's will requires, and they refuse to obey.

> *Nevertheless the men rowed hard to bring it to the land; but they could not: for the sea wrought, and was tempestuous against them.*
>
> — JONAH 1:13

The crew listened to Jonah, but they did not want to throw him overboard. Instead, they tried to escape the storm by rowing. They quickly learned that it was impossible to thwart the will of Sovereign God. How many times have you tried and failed to use your own strength to get out of a storm brought about by your own disobedience?

> *Wherefore they cried unto the LORD, and said, We beseech thee, O LORD, we beseech thee, let us not perish for this man's life, and lay not upon us innocent blood: for thou, O LORD, hast done as it pleased thee.*
>
> — JONAH 1:14

These pagans again exceeded Jonah in their reverence to God. They cried out in prayer to God, pleading for their lives, and asking forgiveness for casting Jonah overboard. Unbelievably, Jonah, God's prophet for that generation, does not even offer up a prayer of his own.

> *"So they took up Jonah, and cast him forth into the sea: and the sea ceased from her raging."*
>
> — JONAH 1:15

This incredible display of God's power, both the sudden arrival and ceasing of the storm, show the severity of God's response to defiance. He sent this storm in response to the sin of one man, and he stopped it immediately when the offender was removed from their midst. America should pay careful attention to the story of Jonah. If God sent a storm as a result of the sin of one prophet, most assuredly He will unleash a tempest against an entire nation that rebels against Him and His ways.

> *Then the men feared the LORD exceedingly, and offered a sacrifice unto the LORD, and made vows.*
>
> — JONAH 1:16

The theme of the heathen crew being more respectful of God than Jonah is woven throughout the first chapter of this book. Once again, we see them responding to God in reverence. They feared the Lord, made sacrifices and offered vows of consecration. It is shocking that these pagans could see the importance of a right relationship with God, but Jonah the prophet could not. Was Jonah so blinded and self-absorbed, in his desire to do his own will, he did not even consider God and His will? Sadly, Jonah sounds like the average American Christian.

The sailors seem to be the only ones paying attention to what God is doing in this story, and they seem to be learning from it. They saw the mistakes of Jonah, and they determined they were not going to make those same mistakes. They learned from the results of Jonah's actions and decided to change their own. My prayer is that

America is as wise as those crewmen and learn from the lessons of Jonah. I pray we would realize the cost of rebellion toward God and honor Him with our lives and commitments. True wisdom is learning from the mistakes of others to avoid the pain and heartache of God's chastening.

Once, while on break from college, I received a phone call that a friend had been in a terrible car accident. He ran into a concrete embankment, and the crash appeared fatal. As I rushed to the hospital, my mind went back to all the times we played basketball together in high school, then to the time when we both surrendered to God's call to preach the Gospel. We went to the same Bible college to prepare for our calling. As the memories played, my thoughts returned to the time he told me he was dropping out of Bible college to pursue a degree in another field. Over the following months, we grew apart, attending different schools and pursuing different vocations. Now I raced to the hospital to see him for perhaps the last time.

The bloody mess they told me was my friend is a memory that I will never forget. It was as if some horrible twist of fate replaced my high school friend with a mangled piece of flesh, kept alive by a ventilator. As I helplessly listened to noise of wires, beeps, and machine-induced breaths, I could not drown out the thought that my friend would never leave this room alive.

Contrary to the doctors prognosis, he survived. After many

months of rehabilitation, he came home, and even returned to school. He soon abandoned his pursuits in medicine and returned to Bible college to resume his pastoral studies.

Sometime later, while riding together, he turned to me and said, "It wasn't an accident."

"What?" I was not quite sure what he meant.

"It wasn't an accident. I deliberately ran into that concrete embankment because I was miserable and running from God."

My high school friend is in the ministry today serving God as a pastor. He survived his trip to Tarshish, but he did not escape unscathed. Today he is fulfilling God's call for his life, but he does so with severe arthritis and a pronounced limp. He would forewarn everyone reading this book, "Don't run from God's call! Please, don't run from God's call! The consequences of your rebellion will haunt you for a lifetime. Please, do not run from God's call!"

America, please do not run from God's call.

GOD'S PRESCRIPTION FOR A SICK SOCIETY

I am a firm believer in the power of gratitude. I find it rejuvenating to take a deep breath and a few moments to consider all the ways I have been blessed. Nothing feeds a spirit of gratitude more than reflecting upon the goodness of God in my life. When assessing my life, I quickly realize that God has smiled on me with good health. I am rarely sick, and apart from blood pressure medication, I have no daily prescription regimen. While I am glad I do not have to take a list of medicines, I know they have their place. On the rare occasion that I do get sick, I am always thankful to hear the doctor say, "I know just what you need" as he writes out a prescription. It is comforting to know there is someone who, as an authority on the subject, can see just what I need and tell me how to recover.

Just as the doctor does during physical sickness, God

provides a remedy for His children when they are spiritually sick. In the book of Second Chronicles, God gives counsel to the nation of Israel regarding their condition. They suffer from the symptoms of drought and famine. God identifies their sin as the cause and provides consultation to alleviate their present suffering and lead to their ultimate cure.

Healing is not about taking the body to a state beyond that which it was designed. Healing is about restoring systems to their optimal operating capacity. As believers, we understand all sickness is a result of the fallen state of man. Sin keeps our bodies from experiencing the perfect health that God's original design intended. Thus, healing is the body's return to its originally designed state. This is why the study of anatomy and biology is foundational for the education of a medical professional. To facilitate healing, one must recognize the original correct condition.

When it comes to America, healing can only come when we recognize the original conditions of our foundation. Despite what has been purported by modern secularists, America is the only nation on earth built directly upon the Christian faith. From the Charter of Rhode Island invoking the blessing of God to the Articles of Confederation of New England declaring the colonies' goal as the advancement of the Kingdom, to the Charter of Carolina proclaiming "zeal for the propagation of the Christian faith," Christianity is irrevocably embedded in the foundation of this nation.

This allegiance to God has been paramount in the United States throughout its existence, and that piety has undeniably brought the favor of God. Civilizations follow a predictable arc of rise and fall that can often be brutally rapid. Among the most prolific civilizations in history, the average length of the cycle has been two centuries. If the life expectancy of humans is seventy to eighty years, then it could be said the life expectancy of a nation is two hundred years.

Throughout my time in the ministry, I have seen many people live beyond the "average" life expectancy, and some outlived the prognosis of doctors based upon their health. Many of them use the phrase to describe their life beyond the expected, calling it "living on borrowed time."

In light of our understanding of the average nation lasting two hundred years, America is living on borrowed time. Not only has America exceeded the average, it has also fallen into societal sickness, having drifted far from the intentions of its Founding Fathers. America's condition brings to mind the tale of the man who leaped from the roof of a tall building. About halfway down the building he passed an open window and was heard saying, "Everything is going along pretty well so far." How foolish to be hurtling toward death, but comforted by the moment.

Has there ever been a more apt description of America? At breakneck speed, America is racing toward destruction, but people are lulled into a state of empty peace because things are not all that bad right now. Friends, America is falling. We are falling morally. We are falling spiritually. We are falling governmentally. We are falling. Is there hope in the midst of this fall? Is there a cure for what ails us?

There is hope, but it will require that we submit to the prescribed treatment. Unfortunately, nations often treat their problems like individuals treat their ailments. Humans have a tendency to think if they just ignore their problems, things will get better on their own. This strategy is ineffective for sick people, and it will not work for a sick America. If we are going to recover from our national infirmity, we must submit to God's plan of treatment. You will not find this plan in the latest medical textbook. Rather, this plan can be found in the Second Book of Chronicles. America's hope for wholeness is prescribed there, but will we follow the instructions?

> *If I shut up heaven that there be no rain, or if I command the locusts to devour the land, or if I send pestilence among my people;*
>
> — 2 CHRONICLES 7:13

One of the hardest decisions many people will ever make is whether or not to submit to a doctor's treatment plan.

Perhaps a medical regimen has a high risk of side effects that produce suffering rivaling the disease. Maybe the treatment is still being developed and results can not be guaranteed. Whatever the specifics, many times treatment decisions seem like the patient is just choosing which way of suffering they like best. Simply put, sometimes things that are good for you can be difficult to accept and even cause much pain.

Verse 13 deals with such a treatment: God's chastening. No one really likes to be disciplined, but we like the results of discipline. The same is true in spiritual matters. God's correction can be difficult, but rest assured, God disciplines His children.

As a child, I can remember times when I had misbehaved, but perhaps due to our surroundings, my parents could not fully administer discipline at that moment. I am sure I am not the only child that heard the phrase, "Just wait till we get home!" A promise of coming punishment is never enjoyable, but sometimes that promise is enough to move us to repentance. Here in Second Chronicles, God makes a promise of discipline that includes a coming drought, a devouring by insects, and disease in the land.

Although it reads like three punishments, you can see the three "stages" of the correction build upon one another. The arrival of dryness will create lack and hunger. An insect infestation destroying crops would also lead to famine, starvation, and death. God also speaks of disease coming upon the land, in a time when rampant sickness could easily become a plague that would kill thousands. Will it take all these things to wake up God's children? Sadly, these things did happen, and the people simply continued living the way they had been, never realizing God was trying to stir them.

We are no different. Do we ever ask why hardships have come upon us? When communities or nations go through droughts, do we ask if God is judging our disobedience? When we have modern day pestilence, which often shows up as economic collapse, do we ask whether or not God is displeased with us? When sickness, including the plague of mental health issues we are facing, sweeps through the nation, do we ask ourselves if it is a result of our sin? If we are not asking these questions, we ought to be.

For some, the idea of God's chastening contradicts their idea of a loving God. However, to a person who has studied the nature of God, these chastening events come not from a vengeful God, but a loving God that seeks His children's return to healthy fellowship with Him.

No doubt, when you read the words of II Chronicles 7:14, you find them familiar. There are the oft-quoted, albeit quickly forsaken, refrain of many a religious leader, particularly after a time of national tragedy. Nonetheless, despite the trite way that this Scripture has been used, it actually contains a prescription that God promises will bring wholeness to a nation.

PRIDE MUST BE ASSAULTED

If my people, which are called by my name, shall humble themselves ...

— 2 CHRONICLES 7:14

When God begins a work, He will begin it with His own people. This certainly runs contrary to the way we as believers often react to situations. Christians are quick to blame the Republicans, or the Democrats, or the independents, the schools, the courts, the media, or whoever else we deem a convenient scapegoat for the subject at hand. Yet, when God begins dealing with a nation, He begins not with the halls of Congress, but in the pews and boardrooms of the church.

The principles found in this promise show us America's greatest problems are not with its politicians or entertainers, but with the backslidden Christians in the pew. If divine judgment is to be averted, the church in America must return to a life of obedience and unreserved devotion to God. The nation will never be corrected until the body of Christ corrects itself.

The opening round of God's prescription is a dose of humility. The Scripture instructs healing begins with humbling yourself before God. No matter the arena of life, you will never be able to improve until you first humble yourself. Pride prevents progress. Pride places a higher value on ourselves than our value of God. Pride leads a person to say, "I know more than God about running my life, raising my kids, determining my priorities, or anything else for that matter." You will not accept help or guidance from anyone, God included, if you think you know better than them.

Simply put, God will not reside where He does not reign.

Pride causes an individual to disregard counsel, including God's. Pride is what caused Satan to be cast out of heaven. Self-exaltation led him to believe his opinions and desires were equal with God's, and God could not let that go unchecked. The pride-inspired rebellion of Satan provoked a sudden and replete reaction from God. God cast Satan from His presence. It was incredibly foolish for Satan to disregard the power of God and exalt himself, but it is no less foolish when we give no credence to God's Word and instead pursue our own haughty desires.

Pride is the root condition of any trespass against God, and that is why God reserves a special hatred for the sin of pride. Pride is so assured of its own abilities it will not seek the counsel of God in His Word. Pride is so sufficient in its own self it neglects the corporate worship and the accountability that connection to a local church brings. Pride needs no advice, so it fails to seek God in prayer. Pride is insidious to man and a stench in the nostrils of Almighty God. Sadly, American Christianity is reeking of pride's hellish odor.

The only counter to pride is for the believer to intentionally embrace humility. The word *humble* means to bend the knee in submission, which speaks of voluntarily placing oneself under the authority of another. We can never expect a move of God in a place where there is no submission to God. Simply put, God will not reside where He does not reign.

The sixth chapter of Mark tells of a place that limited the move of God through their pride and unbelief. Should we think that America will be any different? This thought process is why we ought to ask the hard questions when chastening comes, or when revival seems to evade us. Is God trying to tell us something? Is there some sin in our churches, our community, or our nation that God is instructing us to correct? More often than not, pride trips us again, and rather than examining ourselves we explain away chastening as coincidence.

PRAYER MUST BE APPROPRIATED

> *If my people, which are called by my name, shall humble themselves, and pray ...*
>
> — 2 CHRONICLES 7:14

Self-sufficiency has been the end of many a leader and nation. Pride has a way of blinding an individual to his own weakness. In Christianity, this incorrect valuation of one's abilities leads to a neglect of prayer. Prayerlessness is intertwined with pride because prayerlessness results from a heart that does not believe it needs to call on the help of the Lord.

We have all heard actions speak louder than words, and the same is true of a prayerless life. Prayerlessness makes the statement, "I am all I need." The person who does not pray is declaring they are self-sufficient, and they can depend on their own abilities and assets to provide what they need. Prayerlessness is pride on display, and it brings swift condemnation from God.

Pride is a destroyer. Pride leads to prayerlessness, and prayerlessness results in powerlessness. Satan needs not fear the strongest saint on their feet, but he trembles at the sight of the weakest believer on their knees. Satan knows the results of prayer. God bestows His power upon praying people. The prophet Samuel was born because Hannah prayed him into existence. A layman by the name of Nehemiah prayed, and God empowered him to rebuild the walls of his home. The church gathered in an upper room prayer meeting, and thousands were saved when God's power was poured out. Even a pagan nation found herself converted and spared from destruction when Nineveh came to God in prayer. There is power in prayer!

We are so quick to celebrate the potential power of prayer, but we so often neglect to see the potential realized through the practice of prayer. You certainly are keenly aware of the promises associated with prayer, but how is your prayer life? If prayer is lacking in your life, you have a pride problem. That may be a hard pill to swallow, but it is a necessary one. The only reason you neglect prayer is because you believe more in your own gifts and abilities than you do in God's gifts and abilities.

The problem with operating in your own abilities is you are completely incapable of making any real impact in areas that involve spiritual strongholds. The effects of prayerless Christianity can be seen throughout America. Rampant drug addiction, the explosion of violence, and unprecedented immorality are all signs of a society whose church has lost its power. The only way to see a reversal of these maladies is for the church to be restored to a place of power through the move of God. The only way that will be seen is if the church returns to steadfast prayer.

PRIORITIES MUST BE ALIGNED

If my people, which are called by my name, shall humble themselves, and pray, and seek my face...

— 2 CHRONICLES 7:14

I cannot count the times I have heard people speak of God having turned his back upon America. However, the Bible teaches that God draws nigh to those who draw nigh to him. In other words, we have forsaken Him He has not forsaken us. Thus, after pride is dealt with, the next prescription deals with the priority of seeking God.

The word *seek* means to search with great diligence, persistence, intensity, and focus. In order to seek God, you must first turn toward Him and away from sin. This turning happens when a person repents of his rebellion and transfers his desire from sin to God. God desires His people seek closeness above all else. The seeking heart beats not only to know about God but to know Him in a deep and intimate way.

Seeking God requires a level of dedication greater than any other life pursuit. How different would your life look if you were as diligent in advancing in your walk with God as you are in advancing in your career? What if you sought out God with the same fervor you employ to track down the latest episode of your favorite show? What if you followed God like you follow your favorite sports team? What really is your number one priority?

When anything other than God is the top priority in your life, Scripture says you are guilty of idolatry. God must be first because God alone is worthy to be first! If you realize something other than God has become your primary focus, you must quickly repent of your misplaced worship. Humbly invite your Father back to His rightful place atop your life's priorities.

PURITY MUST BE AFFIRMED

> *If my people, which are called by my name, shall humble themselves, and pray, and seek my face, and turn from their wicked ways ...*
>
> — 2 CHRONICLES 7:14

As I remarked at the beginning of the chapter, I have been blessed with good health for most of my life. However, there have been a few times I have been on antibiotics for some ailment. Any time I have ever been prescribed an antibiotic, it came with specific instructions to ensure I took the correct dosage. In fact, stopping an antibiotic regimen early can result in a return of the infection in greater force than the original sickness.

Just like with my antibiotics, this prescription from God is one we must be sure to completely apply. Having addressed pride and priorities, God now brings our attention to purity. The word *turn* is frequently translated *repent* and means to do an about-face, or turn to head in the opposite direction. Thus, the phrase "turn from their wicked ways" is self-explanatory. God does not want His people living sinfully!

The admonition here is for Christians to examine ourselves, identify anything that does not please the Lord, and eliminate those things from our lives. God will not dwell in a place polluted by the filth of sin. If we expect to see a response to our prayers, our change of priority must include practicing repentance.

The choice is really very simple. You can either forsake sin and once again see God's blessing upon your life, or you can continue to live in sin and watch as destruction and condemnation come upon you. Although many claim Jesus as their Savior while living a sinful lifestyle, the reality is they cannot reject the commands of God without reaping the condemnation of God. Yet, many are trying to do just that.

American Christians lack a full understanding of the severity of sin. Something is terribly wrong when people sing in the choir on Sunday and by Monday use gossip to tear down the church in which they just sang. Something is horribly amiss when a man can teach a Sunday School Class on Sunday morning and then sit in front of the television or computer screen and fill his mind with filth that same evening. Somehow, the church has forgotten God takes notice of our actions and consequences are a reality.

This lackadaisical approach to purity is the single greatest obstacle to revival in this nation or any nation. Sin, hidden and unconfessed hinders any possibility of a spiritual awakening in our land. The only way we will ever see a move of God is if godly sorrow leads to humble repentance before Him.

Clearly, this repentance must begin with Christians. America will never get right with God until the Christians within her borders get right with Him! As the Psalmist wrote, our prayers are hindered when we "regard iniquity." However, there is hope in the verse. If we turn from our sins, God promises to send healing to our land.

> *If my people, which are called by my name, shall humble themselves, and pray, and seek my face, and turn from their wicked ways; then will I hear from heaven, and will forgive their sin, and will heal their land.*
>
> — 2 CHRONICLES 7:14

There is a keyword in the verse, a hinge upon which we the condition of the nation turns. The word is *then*. When we deal with our pride, return to prayer, prioritize God, and seek purity, God promises that His healing will come. We are faced with a choice as a country. We will position ourselves either for God to hear and heal or for Him to confront and condemn. Wrath or favor, blessing or cursing, mercy or chastening, the choice is ours. The only question is whether or not we are willing to follow God's prescription in order to find our healing.

Before a nation can be healed, the people must be changed on an individual level. Perhaps, this is a good place for you to do a thorough self-examination. Prayerfully consider the following questions?

1. Pride: Are there any areas of your life that are not submitted to God? Are there any practices, habits, or choices that do not line up with God's Word?
2. Prayer: Is your life lacking in regular focused prayer? Do you find yourself seeking the counsel of others, but not talking to God about those same situations?
3. Priority: Do you have anything in your life that claims more of your free time than your relationship with God? Do you watch TV or surf the internet with more regularity than you read the Bible and pray?
4. Purity: Are you participating in things which you

know God is not pleased? Is there any hidden sin in your life? Do you find yourself defending things you know God is not pleased with?

Friend, if you answered yes to any of the above questions, now would be a great time to set this book aside and spend a few moments in prayer. Your participation in God's work in healing the land depends upon your proximity to Him. The prescription has been written, now the patients must choose to follow the instructions.

WANTED

I grew up in Atlanta, Georgia and lived there during the time of what was known as the Atlanta Child Murders. From 1979 to 1981, a serial killer wreaked havoc on the city. I recall a palpable fear seemed to spread after the news reports. Warnings to keep an eye on your children and grocery store conversations about the latest murder became a regular part of life. Most disturbing was this killer primarily targeted children. The perpetrator claimed over two dozen victims, many of whom were kidnapped and tortured before being senselessly slaughtered and tossed off bridges or into bodies of water where their remains were found.

During this terrible ordeal, there was a regional and eventually a national manhunt for the sadistic killer who destroyed the peace of our city. No resources were spared, and law enforcement determined to use every means at their disposal to find this evil individual and restore a sense of security to our city.

Ezekiel tells us of another manhunt, a God-ordained manhunt. This search is not for a serial killer, but for a sacred leader God can use to restore righteousness and godliness to a decaying society. However, to understand the need for restoration, we must first understand the conditions of the time.

At the time of Ezekiel chapter 22, Jerusalem was occupied by one of the greatest enemies in its history, the Babylonian Empire. In 606 BC, the Babylonians defeated the Israelites and carried off much of their population as slaves in Babylon, including the prophet Daniel. Almost a decade later in 597 BC, the Babylonians again invaded Israel and carried away a second group of Hebrews as slaves. Ezekiel, a priest in his mid-twenties God would eventually call as a prophet, was in this group.

The total destruction of Jerusalem would not come until 586 BC. Meanwhile, God, in His abounding mercy, extended an opportunity for his people to repent of their ways and avoid this coming doom. Using the prophet Ezekiel, Jehovah issued a call for His children to return to obedience, abandon wickedness, and live lives of submitted holiness. In Chapter 22 of Ezekiel, God uses the prophet as a prosecuting attorney to fully lay out his case against Jerusalem. Ezekiel describes in detail the detestable actions of Jerusalem that were the cause of its society's downfall.

This point is a monumental moment, whereby God brings charges against Jerusalem for her ungodly ways. To fully grasp the substance of God's actions, we must understand the historical and spiritual significance of Jerusalem. More than just a great city, Jerusalem was the center of spiritual activity for God's people. The psalmist referred to Jerusalem as the city of God, a city that was to be the model to the rest of the world of how to operate in religious and political matters. However, despite its mandate to exemplify itself as a holy place, the people of Jerusalem had drifted far from God's purpose for them. The wickedness of their ways brought God's chastening, and their persistent lack of repentance led to their destruction.

THE DECAYING SOCIETY

Ezekiel, God's prosecutor, opens his arguments against Jerusalem with an indictment of its decaying culture. Sin permeated the society, and God could not let that wickedness stand. Lest the people fain ignorance, Ezekiel clearly identifies the culprits to their condition.

> *There is a conspiracy of her prophets in the midst thereof, like a roaring lion ravening the prey; they have devoured souls; they have taken the treasure and precious things; they have made her many widows in the midst thereof.*
>
> — EZEKIEL 22:25

First, the prosecutor sets his gaze upon the prophets. Charged with the responsibility as God's spokesmen, the prophets should denounce the wickedness in their society. They had instead become deceivers, devouring and defrauding the people. They should stand against oppression, but they, in conspiracy with the wicked, protected the oppressors in their sin and even justified their ungodly behavior. Roaring out threats like lions, the prophets made themselves masters over the people and ruled them with oppression and manipulation.

Those who were supposed to be representatives of justice became the exact opposite. They were complicit in the shedding of innocent blood. They greedily contributed to wrongdoing and even caused women to become destitute widows through their cooperation with the evildoers. These prophets persecuted any who dare stand against their false proclamations, destroying anyone who would not submit.

> *And her prophets have daubed them with untempered morter,*

seeing vanity, and divining lies unto them, saying, Thus saith the Lord GOD, when the LORD hath not spoken.

— EZEKIEL 22:28

When God called these prophets, he intended for them to be the moral conscience and spiritual leaders of the nation. However, instead of denouncing sin, they whitewashed or ignored it. Ordained to be bearers of God's truth, they instead dealt in false prophecies and lies. More interested in pleasing men than God, they sold out. Ezekiel points the finger at the prophets and declares God's strong displeasure with their ways.

Her priests have violated my law, and have profaned mine holy things: they have put no difference between the holy and profane, neither have they shewed difference between the unclean and the clean, and have hid their eyes from my sabbaths, and I am profaned among them.

— EZEKIEL 22:26

Of all the officials with a responsibility to holiness, the priests were foremost. They bore the responsibility of teaching God's law and guarding the purity of the temple. The priests were sanctioned to maintain the demarcation between the clean and the unclean.

Instead of fulfilling their responsibility with integrity, the priests joined the prophets in allowing themselves to be swayed by popular opinion. They distorted the line between holy and profane, failing to instruct the people in the ways of God or to enforce the statutes of His law. Abandoning God's precepts, they turned a blind eye to the sin and corruption invading their land. Seeking political correctness over righteousness, they pleased the people by blurring the lines between right and wrong. Tragically, many pastors and church leaders do the same thing today in America.

Not only did the priests fail to address the sins of the society around them, they also abdicated their duty to keep the temple holy. Their failure to teach the people the fundamentals of the faith eroded their moral values and the spiritual climate in God's house.

Reading this, you may wonder what the actions of some priests who lived thousands of years ago have to do with you. Friend, you must realize as a follower of Christ, you have been made a priest. You carry the same expectations as the priests of Jerusalem in the guardianship of purity and holiness in your home and society. Peter tells us that we are "a chosen generation, a royal priesthood, a holy nation."

> *You carry the same expectations as the priests of Jerusalem in the guardianship of purity and holiness...*

The very nature of God demands a separation between right and wrong. God uses his people in every period and culture to demonstrate this distinction to the world. The priests in Ezekiel's day did not live up to their spiritual obligation. An honest evaluation of today's Christians reveals we are failing miserably in our role as priests as well. The church, called to guard against wickedness infiltrating its ranks, has instead celebrated and promoted things that God clearly forbids. Ezekiel points the finger at the priests of his time and ours and declares God displeasure.

Her princes in the midst thereof are like wolves ravening the prey, to shed blood, and to destroy souls, to get dishonest gain.

— EZEKIEL 22:27

Ezekiel shifts his focus from the religious to the secular in addressing the princes. Princes in this time were appointed government officials. In Jerusalem, these officials made great proclamations of hope and prosperity, but the reality of their actions rarely lived up to their rhetoric. Although they were purported to be the servants of the people, they had no real concern for their citizens. Instead, these politicians sought only their own gain, making the people victims of their self-serving actions. Ezekiel, God's prosecutor, compares them to wolves attacking and mutilating their prey. Wolves, notorious for their fierce fighting and cruelty, were an apt picture of the vicious nature and ravenous greed of these leaders.

This description of government officials has striking contemporary parallels. Every election cycle, politicians, and aspiring leaders promise anything to gain position, but, once they are firmly settled in their seats of power, they run away from the platform that got them elected and sell themselves to the highest bidding special interest group. Let us pray that God will raise up statesmen that stand boldly for truth and refuse to deny their principles. Ezekiel points the finger at the seats of government and pronounces that God is not pleased.

> *The people of the land have used oppression, and exercised robbery, and have vexed the poor and needy: yea, they have oppressed the stranger wrongfully.*
>
> — EZEKIEL 22:29

The people undoubtedly applauded Ezekiel when he decried the prophets, priests, and princes. However, at the next target of his ire, the cheers would cease. Having addressed the problems around them, God's prosecutor now turns his attention to the people themselves. What kind of people would such a failed religious and political system produce? The answer is not pretty, because in matters of morality the people were not far behind their leaders. The citizens of Jerusalem were themselves extortioners, robbers, oppressors, thieves, and murderers. Their society was a showcase of violence, greed, indifference to suffering, and general neglect of the things of God.

The description of the people's sinfulness is spread throughout the twenty-second chapter of Ezekiel. There was no discipline in their homes. They were full of immorality and sexual perversions, including abusing their own children. Crime was out of control in the land. The sickness of corruption had spread from the leadership into the whole of society. Israel was septic with wickedness.

Remember, this is not just any city, this was Jerusalem. This city was the City of God. It was the home of God's people, the location of God's temple, but it was a cesspool of sinful degradation. Their willful depravity was an affront to God who called them to be holy. Because of their sin, they were days away from God-sent destruction.

In earlier chapters, we saw the strong spiritual founding of America. When we view our current condition, we cannot help but see how far we have fallen. Wickedness abounds. Abortion, the murder of innocent children, is legal and promoted in all fifty states of our union. Each year alcohol kills thousands and maims thousands more in vehicular accidents, while four in ten suicides and half of all rapes are alcohol-related. In fact, alcohol kills more people annually than some wars. Yet our government licenses its sale, and it is promoted everywhere in advertising and entertainment.

As wonderful as technology in the age of the internet has been, it has also enabled the insidious flow of pornography. Billions of dollars spent on the ingestion of filth is an indicator of just how far this nation has fallen.

Consider the American Church. American Christianity has become so consumer-driven that churches are more concerned with what people want than what they desperately need. The church has become lazy, complacent, carnal, and prideful. Of course, the church is an outgrowth of pulpits where preachers are more concerned with being entertainers, comedians, and intellectuals than they are with proclaiming God's truth.

The greatest problem in America is not a collapse in the stock market; our greatest problem is sin. America's greatest fear ought not to be Russian infiltration in her elections, but immorality infiltrating her society. America's biggest threat is not from terrorism. America's greatest threat is the judgment of Almighty God. America's hope is not better government, tax cuts, or a stronger military. America's only hope is forsaking sin and turning to God in repentance.

THE DILIGENT SEARCH

> *And I sought for a man among them, that should make up the hedge, and stand in the gap before me for the land, that I should not destroy it: but I found none.*
>
> — EZEKIEL 22:30

God seeks for a man. Ezekiel speaks the word as singular – *one man*. It seems unusual that God seeks for just one person to stem the tide of wickedness and turn the people back to him. Yet, history tells us that institutions, nations, and movements pivot on the actions of one. This fact is true in history and in life.

Babylon was nothing without King Nebuchadnezzar. Persia was hamstrung without Cyrus. Greece may just be a footnote in the annals of history without Alexander the Great. Rome, though a republic, would never have risen to its heights without Caesar.

More recent history of nations and institutions bears testimony to the same pattern. What would England be without Churchill, or America without Lincoln, or the church without Martin Luther?

You cannot overstate the importance of the right person in the right place at the right time. Everywhere, in every age there has been the influence of an individual. For

Jerusalem God gives the city one more chance, but can He find that one person who is willing to volunteer to serve?

A Man of Separation

> *And I sought for a man among them ...*
>
> — EZEKIEL 22:30

God was not looking for merely any man, but a man that would stand up for what was right in a sinful society. To a city whose prophets are cruel, whose priests are compromised, whose princes are corrupt, and whose people are contemptible, God declares that among them is one for which He is looking, one who will stand for the right.

We may be surprised at the thought that God would find a good man in such a place, but God has a track record of doing just that. When the whole earth was filled with violence, God found Noah, and the earth was spared. When the whole earth was idolatrous, God found Abraham and through him, the earth was blessed. When a whole nation was fearful, God found David, and Israel was delivered. When the earth was covered with pagan empires full of heathen practices, God found Paul, and through him, the gospel spread across the globe. God knows how to find His one!

God still seeks men and women today. People of commitment, unafraid to be different, who will respond to God's call and be sanctified for His use. I have written that destruction is coming to America, but it can be stopped. You can stop the destruction. Sir, ma'am, teenager, mom, dad, grandparent, employee, business owner, Christian, YOU can be His one!

A Man of Determination

> *And I sought for a man among them, that should make up the hedge, and stand in the gap ...*
>
> — EZEKIEL 22:30

Ezekiel says God is looking for one who will stand in the gap. The word *gap* can be translated as *breach* such as Nehemiah's reference to a wall with "no breach left in it" or Isaiah's mention of a "repairer of the breach." A breach is a broken down place in the wall. Such a place was a liability, a weak spot where an invading enemy could obtain easy entry to a city.

Spiritually speaking, sin creates breaches in the hedge of protection around God's people. Through those gaps, good leaks out and evil pours in. God has given His followers the mission of being repairers of the breach. He is looking for people who will stand in the gap sin has made and turn back the onslaught of Satan against the church.

Standing in the gap means filling the hole or pouring out your life for the benefit of others. Friends, there are gaps everywhere. Homes, churches, institutions, and governments all have gaps that must be filled. Sin has made greater breaches than we have ever seen. Who will repair the breach? Who will plant their feet on the truth of God and defy every lie the enemy throws against us? Who will be His one? Will you?

A MAN OF SUPPLICATION

> *...before me for the land, that I should not destroy it...*
>
> — EZEKIEL 22:30

God was not looking for a king, warrior, prophet, priest, or prince. He was looking for an intercessor. A beautiful picture of intercession is found in the text. The way we stand in the gap, the way we hold back the judgments of God, is through repentance and intercession. When God comes forth to pour out His wrath on the sinful, intercession can cause Him to refrain.

A prolific example of intercession is found in Exodus. While Moses was away meeting with God, the people had made a golden calf and danced naked around it. God's people worshiped a heathen idol in a heathen manner. God took one look at their transgression and determined that He would destroy them. He even told Moses to stand aside and let Him pour out His wrath upon Israel, and God would raise up a new nation out of his seed.

Many people would have stepped away and allowed God to give the Israelites what they had coming to them, especially with the promise of being the patriarch of a new, holy nation. However, Moses' love for his people was resolute. He told God that if Israel could not be spared, then he did not want to live. If they were going to blotted out of God's book of life, he wanted to be blotted out also. Moses stood in the breach for the people.

Unfortunately, there was no Moses, nor Noah, nor Abraham for Jerusalem. The verse finishes with some of the saddest words in the Old Testament, "but I found none."

THE DISASTROUS SLAUGHTER

> *Therefore have I poured out mine indignation upon them; I have consumed them with the fire of my wrath: their own way have I recompensed upon their heads, saith the Lord GOD.*
>
> — EZEKIEL 22:31

Many ministers point out the amazing, albeit tragic, fact that God would have spared Sodom and Gomorrah if He could have found ten righteous men among them. Jerusalem's story is even more incredible than Sodom's.

Jerusalem would have been spared if God could have found just one righteous man, but tragically, He found none. Not in the entirety of God's city, in the ranks of God's prophets, nor in the courts of God's priests could one person be found who would respond to the call to stand in the gap. Not one person had enough compassion to sacrifice for the souls in the city. Not one was courageous enough to risk affliction by standing for righteousness.

It was a terrible reality that this great city housed no one with enough backbone to go against the culture; no one consecrated enough to live in total surrender to God. Even so, we should take a good look at our nation in its current state. There are gaps everywhere. Gaps have been created by Christians who died without a new generation rising to their level of dedication. Gaps have been created by Christians who, like Demas, for love of worldly things have turned their backs on God and His Will. Gaps have been created by Christians who have grown weary of the weight of the cross and have, perhaps even unintentionally, neglected their walk.

Someone has let the enemy pierce the wall of our faith. Someone, some "one", His one, must fill the void. Jerusalem was destroyed, but not because God lacked mercy. God's mercy and long-suffering were abundant. Jerusalem was destroyed because God could not find ONE who would intercede, ONE who would stand for right, ONE who would be His one.

God's wrath was poured out on Jerusalem for lack of one. The temple was destroyed for lack of one. The people were dragged into captivity for lack of one. Will America also be destroyed for lack of one? Will you be the "one" in your world, your family, your church, your community? God is still searching for one.

New York City's corner at Fulton and William Street was the home of the old Dutch Reformed Church. Jeremiah Landfear, a layman, had seen the decline of the church as the impoverished and depleted community around it deteriorated. As he walked the streets of the city, Jeremiah saw hopelessness in nearly every face.

There was a particularly noticeable anxiety among the businessmen. The nation was on the precipice of an economic collapse, and they knew it. Knowing God was the only hope of any people, Jeremiah decided to start a prayer meeting and circulated hundreds of fliers. On the first Wednesday of September at 12 o'clock, Jeremiah sat in the third-floor assembly room in the North Dutch Reformed Church on Fulton Street.

He was alone.

Five minutes passed, then ten, fifteen. Now twenty minutes had gone by and he remained alone. At thirty minutes past the hour, he heard footsteps on the stairs. Then more. Then more. Finally, five men joined him in prayer.

The next Wednesday, twenty businessmen were present,

the next week thirty. Those men made an agreement to meet every day. On the first day, one hundred men gathered to pray, and amazingly, many of them were not Christians. In three months the prayer meeting had grown until every room in that old North Dutch Reformed church was overflowing with praying men. The auditorium, classrooms, and even the basement were full. Every room and every corner were so filled that many resorted to praying outside.

The prayer meeting, having outgrown the location, they decided to expand to the John's Street Methodist Church around the corner. The first day it opened, it was filled with praying men. Burton's theater, located downtown, opened for prayer at noon. On its first day, a newspaper reported, "It was stuffed from pit to dome." The Fire Marshall showed up and turned away men who had come to pray. Within six months, fifty thousand New Yorkers were gathering for daily prayer at one hundred and fifty locations spread throughout the city. Twenty-five thousand businessmen came to Christ. It became commonplace to see upwards of one hundred people respond to a single invitation to receive Christ in churches around the city.

The revival did not end in New York City. Streams flowed outward to the surrounding areas, sweeping across Long Island and even reaching to Albany, where twelve hundred conversions were reported. Ships coming into port would report when they got within a few miles of shore, an inexplicable conviction would grip the hearts of those on board. Whole crews were converted, including at least thirty ship captains. Within a year and a half, well over a million people came to know Christ, and it all started with one person's commitment to intercession.

Through the efforts of one man, God shook a nation. God is still looking for one. One to stand in the gap. One to intercede. One to get a burden. God has used one before, and He will use one again. Are you the one He is searching for?

HOPE FOR A HOPELESS SOCIETY

Every year in America, millions of dollars are spent producing awards shows. The public cannot seem to get enough of these events as they watch for hours, tuning in for the red carpet arrivals and staying up late for the post-show comments. Every professional sport has a hall of fame, and each year the world applauds the newest crop of standout inductees. The recipients of these accolades, and even those simply considered for them, are treated as royalty wherever they go. People flock to them by the thousands, hoping for a glimpse, a touch, an autograph, or the elusive selfie with a "great" person.

America is obsessed with the idea of greatness. Every day on television and the internet, there are discussions going on ranking the greatness of everyone from athletes to politicians to entertainers. Yet despite our infatuation with the idea of greatness, we have a confused sense of what true greatness actually is. We toss the term "great" around like candy without really considering the individual we call great. Not only are we presumptuous to think of ourselves authorities on human greatness, but we are not even adept in our appraisals.

Does a sports star embody greatness based upon their skill or athletic ability? Is a businessman great when he operates a thriving business in a booming city? Is he really great, or did he just happen to be in the right place at the right time? A person who loves to hunt may become quite skilled, but is he truly a great hunter, or is he simply knowledgeable about his hobby? Are there any truly "great" people in these groups, or are they simply blessed with God-given abilities and providential opportunity?

Perhaps we are unqualified to be the judges of greatness in life, for our view of greatness is quite limited in its scope and perspective. The only one who could truly declare what is great would have to be the greatest. Anselm and many philosophers since have called God the "supremely great being." This is a fitting description for God, who is the embodiment of true greatness. Thus, when God ascribes greatness, He does so being fully qualified. With His perfect perspective of time, space, and matter, He alone can determine the quality of anything and whether or not it rightfully can be called great.

Understanding God is uniquely qualified to ascribe worth makes it all the more noteworthy when He does. In the third chapter of Jonah, God labels Nineveh as a great city, and it becomes the location of a great revival. In fact, if there were a show or website that ranked the greatest revivals of all time, the revival at Nineveh may take the top spot. A discussion of great revivals would certainly include the Great Awakenings, the Welsh Revival, the Shantung Revival. In the New Testament, the revival that followed Pentecost, where the Holy Spirit was poured out on the disciples and in one day three thousand were saved, would probably take the top prize.

However, Jonah tells us even more people were saved under the Old Testament Prophet's ministry in Nineveh than were saved at Pentecost. The Nineveh revival did not just impact a portion of the population, but it changed an entire metropolis. After Jonah preached and the Holy Spirit moved upon the hearts of the people, the entire city turned to follow God. Now, that is a great revival!

A GREAT MESSAGE FROM GOD

> *And the word of the LORD came unto Jonah the second time, saying,*

— JONAH 3:1

Who lost the Super Bowl two years ago? Who is the second-best swimmer behind Michael Phelps? Who is the number two boxer of all time? Who is that with the silver medal? Who is the second greatest pitcher in all of baseball history? Who caught the second biggest fish? Who cares?

You are never going to turn on the TV or scroll through your Facebook feed and see an ad for a show or article revealing who is second best at anything. Ordinarily, the word "second" is a bad word. When my family plays board games, we torment the second place "winner" by naming them first loser. Second place is simply not a desirable result for most people. Second place means you were not quite good enough. You came close, but someone was simply better.

Jonah experiences a "second" in this verse, but his is certainly not a negative second. In fact, his "second" is incredibly positive because his second is a God-given second chance. The Word of God came to Jonah the first time, and he failed; now God has extended another opportunity for Jonah to do the right thing. As much as we may despise second place, we sure do need second chances.

Truth be told, there is a little Jonah DNA in all of us. No matter our position or past successes, everyone has at one time or another needed a second chance after terribly missing the mark on our first. In those times of failure, it is consolatory to know that God is a God of second chances. Although that may sound trite, it is no empty cliché. The Bible gives us many examples of first-time failures that God turned into second-chance successes.

From Adam in Genesis to Samson in Judges to David in the fifty-first Psalm, to Luke's account of the prodigal son, again and again, we see that God gives second chances. Peter became a great leader after his second chance. John Mark became an indispensable help to the church after his second chance. You are reading this book today because somewhere in your past God gave you a second chance.

> *Arise, go unto Nineveh, that great city, and preach unto it the preaching that I bid thee.*
>
> — JONAH 3:2

The first time Jonah was called by God to go to Nineveh he rebelled and ended up with a whale of a problem. Here, God comes with the same call: literally word-for-word the same. God's plan and purpose for Jonah never changed, even through Jonah's rebellion. Thus, after the chastening, we see the exact same command. How wonderful it is God does not throw away His plans for us. Even when we do not listen like we should, He calls and calls again.

The beauty of God's grace is even more evident when we

realize how little of it we deserve. Yes, we have heard it said that everyone deserves a second chance, but no one really deserves a second chance. Second chances are not justice, they are grace. Nonetheless, we all can be grateful God in His abundant grace gives second chances when we do not deserve them.

> God's plan and purpose for Jonah never changed, even through Jonah's rebellion.

A GREAT MISSION FIELD FROM GOD

Arise, go unto Nineveh, that great city, and preach unto it the preaching that I bid thee.

— JONAH 3:2

Nineveh was an impressive city in many ways, and even God called it "that great city." It was as powerful a city as existed anywhere in the world at this time. Its walls, standing one hundred feet tall and wide enough for chariots to race three wide atop, housed a population of well over a million people. The people could rest easy under the vigilant eyes standing guard in Nineveh's twelve hundred watchtowers, each standing two hundred feet tall. Nevertheless, all was not well, for Nineveh, great in power and population, was exceedingly wicked.

Nineveh's notorious ferocity and heinous immorality did not happen by chance. This kind of pervasive evil is cultivated. For Nineveh, the root of their wickedness was in their idolatrous worship of Baal and Ishtar. Devotion to their gods led them to offer their own children as human sacrifices to gain favor with these false deities.

Not surprisingly, considering they were willing to sacrifice their own children, the people of Nineveh were known for extreme brutality. They would skin enemies alive, and then hang the skins on their walls as trophies. They were known to decapitate enemies and pile the rotting heads outside the city gates as a warning to aspiring opponents. The enemies they did not kill, they took captive, parading them with hooks in their noses like captured livestock. You can understand why Jonah did not want to travel to this city and declare the Word of God.

Yet, despite their sinfulness, God was no less committed to Nineveh than He was to Jonah. While Jonah saw only evildoers, God saw the people in Nineveh as souls He wanted to save. God's desire has not changed since the days of Jonah. He still yearns to save the most brutal, wicked, and vile people in our world. He is the same yesterday, today, and forever, as is His unfailing compassion for the most nefarious among us.

However, like Jonah, we often resist God's desire to show mercy to the exceedingly sinful people around us. Even so, God has given us the mandate to carry the gospel to the lost. You have been strategically placed in the mission fields of your job, your family, and your community. Your mission is simply to share the message of God's love with those in your world. Just as Jonah was specifically called, you are divinely appointed. Are you responding to that appointment? What will it take to get you to share the gospel with your mission field? Hopefully, unlike Jonah, you will not need a storm.

A GREAT MANDATE FROM GOD

Arise, go unto Nineveh, that great city, and preach unto it the preaching that I bid thee.

— JONAH 3:2

God's desire to save the lost has not changed from the Old Testament to the New, or from the time of Nineveh to the time of America. Neither has God's command to his followers changed. The New Testament records Timothy receiving the same instructions as Jonah: "Preach the Word." The job of the minister is not to proclaim his own thoughts and ideas, but to declare the very thoughts and ideas of God recorded in His Word. God gave Jonah the exact message He expected him to declare, and He has done the same for us. God expects us like He expected Jonah, to deliver the message of His Word boldly, not fearing the response we may encounter.

> *And Jonah began to enter into the city a day's journey, and he cried, and said, Yet forty days, and Nineveh shall be overthrown.*
>
> — JONAH 3:4

In the world of preaching, acclaim is often reserved for the speakers who address the largest crowds or pastor the church with the nicest facilities. However, the most challenging of preaching tasks is not in the pulpit, but on the street corner. Street preaching is a difficult venture. Trying to proclaim the Word of God to people who did not come to hear it can be a struggle, to say the least. Many will pass by without acknowledging the proclaimers presence, while others will stop and linger only to ridicule the man or the message. Typically, only a few will actually listen, and fewer still will respond. Many men who are lions in the pulpit shrink at the thought of preaching on the street.

As tough as contemporary street preaching is, Jonah's situation was even more difficult. He was a Jewish man preaching on the streets of Nineveh, a city that despised

Jews. Furthermore, if ethnicity was not enough, Jonah hailed from a country that was a hated political rival of the people of Nineveh. Imagine God sending you to a place where you were hated, and that happened to be home to the cruelest and most violent people in the entire world. Imagine having to stand in the center of that city surrounded by hundreds of thousands of malevolents and declare, "God has decreed you are going to be destroyed in forty days, and all of you are going to be in hell. Have a great day." (The belly of a big fish is sounding better all the time!)

This was a seemingly impossible task. One man, prophet or not, was to confront thousands of people with a message of judgment. Apparently, God's chastening had brought Jonah back to a place of submission because he made no attempt to dilute or sweeten the message. No test audience or public relations firm guided his "branding." There was no security detail or protective police presence. Jonah went to the largest, most wicked city in the world and stood before them all, proclaiming exactly what God's Word said.

The secret to Jonah's resolve and the revival that followed was his regard for God above man. Jonah did not focus on the response of the Ninevites, because preaching to please the audience would have made him a slave to their preferences. Jonah was consumed with gaining God's approval more than ministerial success or even his own safety. Too many people God has called grow discouraged and abandon their life's purpose because they are more focused on the response of the masses than the Master. In serving God, you may gain both God's approval and man's, but you cannot pursue both.

Seeking to gain the applause of men has caused many of God's messengers to corrupt His message. These compromising spokesmen often miss the full impact of God's tidings. Jonah's message was a message of judgment and wrath, telling of coming destruction as a result of sin. Yet it was also a message of mercy and love, a presentation of a forty-day gift of God's longsuffering, an offer to repent and find deliverance. To some, the message sounded cruel, but in totality, it was a loving call to experience God's grace.

> *There is always a deadline with God.*

What if God sent a message like that to America? What if He gave our nation forty days until destruction? Forty days to clean up the entertainment that flows into our devices. Forty days to clean up the humanism and anti-God rhetoric in our schools. Forty days to scrub corruption from our government. Forty days to lay open the scandals in our churches. You have forty days to repent of the sin in your land, or you will be destroyed.

We like to view God's longsuffering as eternal, but God's message came with a deadline. There is always a deadline with God. God does not eternally strive with man. We do not have forever to get right with Him. Sinners do not have forever to repent. Believers do not have forever to submit to God's will for their lives. God is forever, but our time is not. We must respond with urgency while there is still time.

Some have said the wheels of God's wrath do not turn fast, but they are always turning. Noah preached one hundred twenty years before the flood waters wreaked havoc. That is a long time, but it did come to an end. There was a deadline, but the people did not know when the deadline would come. Friends, we do not know when our deadline or our nation's deadline will come. But rest assured; God's warnings always come with a deadline.

Deadlines mean destruction follows declaration, but God's grace allows for a time of decision, however short that time may be. The people of Nineveh had forty days to determine their fate, and then destruction came. You cannot control the declaration or the destruction. The only element in which you have a say is your decision. The only time for salvation is the time God gives. Once the deadline arrives, there can be no decisions, only destruction. You have been blessed with a time of decision. God is calling you to submit. What if He gave you forty days to repent of your ways and avoid His judgment? You have a deadline. What decisions do you need to make?

A GREAT MODIFICATION FOR GOD

> *So the people of Nineveh believed God, and proclaimed a fast, and put on sackcloth, from the greatest of them even to the least of them.*
>
> — JONAH 3:5

There have been times I stepped into the pulpit thinking I had the perfect sermon for the hour, while other times I stepped into the pulpit unsure of the response. I have discovered that when it comes to preaching, just obey God. The response cannot be predicted, or sometimes even understood.

Something like this happened to Jonah. When he went to Nineveh, he no doubt imagined a lot of possible responses, most of which included anger and maybe even assassination. However, when he began to preach, something unforeseen began to happen. The people did not fly into a rage and seize him for torture. He was not forced to flee from a fiery mob bent on bloodshed. No, when he preached, the people believed his message. From the king to the princes to the common people, they all turned to the Lord in response to Jonah's message. A spiritual awakening sprang up from the unlikeliest soil. Nineveh experienced revival!

The move of God in Nineveh was not a "revival" in our modern religious sense, which often means a series of church services followed by a predictable returning to mediocre lukewarmness. This revival was one of inward belief that dramatically affected the outward lives of the converted. Laying aside earthly concerns, the city became consumed with spiritual things. They proclaimed a fast to declare their repentance and consecrate themselves to God. These people were not merely signing commitment cards and shaking the preacher's hand. They had been radically changed!

The revival in Nineveh was all the more remarkable because it reached more than a select few that decided to repent and turn to God. Rather, the entire city, from greatest to the least, fasted and even put on sackcloth as an outward show of their inward humility and brokenness before God. Their thoughts shifted from being fashionable or recognized for their wealth and position. Their chief concern became pleasing Jehovah God through their worship of self-abasement and repentance.

For word came unto the king of Nineveh, and he arose from his throne, and he laid his robe from him, and covered him with sackcloth, and sat in ashes.

— JONAH 3:6

Revival among the people is amazing in its own right, but this revival reached all the way to the leadership of the city. The king laid aside his royal garb and joined his people in sackcloth and ashes. Before Jonah's arrival, the king of Nineveh mandated his subjects worship him as a god. Now his decree not only rejected his own deity but crowned Jehovah King of Nineveh. The king determined his government would be submitted to God.

God will not fail to bless anyone who brings themselves into submission to Him. Nations, churches, governments, corporations, institutions, and individuals will repent of their sin and acknowledge the Lordship of God in their lives will be divinely favored. Amazingly, it does not matter how wicked they have been, God still shows forgiveness and favor to those who approach him in humble repentance.

> [7]*And he caused it to be proclaimed and published through Nineveh by the decree of the king and his nobles, saying, Let neither man nor beast, herd nor flock, taste any thing: let them not feed, nor drink water:* [8]*But let man and beast be covered with sackcloth, and cry mightily unto God: yea, let them turn every one from his evil way, and from the violence that is in their hands.*
>
> — JONAH 3:7–8

Repentance may begin with sorrow for one's actions, but it

does not end there. True repentance includes an absolute renunciation of past sin and a commitment to lifestyle change. For Nineveh, this was a revolutionary change on a national level. They had been one of the most heinously violent nations on the face of the earth, but repentance meant abandoning their cruel treatment of captives and sacrificing their children to idols. Repentance was a total renunciation of their prior wickedness. Just like Nineveh, true repentance will cause you to permanently forsake your sin.

~

A GREAT MIRACLE FROM GOD

And God saw their works, that they turned from their evil way; and God repented of the evil, that he had said that he would do unto them; and he did it not.

— JONAH 3:10

Relationships are about responding to one another. Whether in a business, a church, or a marriage, the strength or weakness of a relationship depends on the way each partner reciprocates. In the first four verses of the chapter, we saw Jonah's response to God. The next five verses described Nineveh's response to God. Now, in the last verse, we see God responding to Nineveh.

It has been said God does not change, people do. God always favors submission and chastens rebellion. Jonah is the poster boy for that truth. He endured misery when he said "no" to God, but he found favor when he acquiesced to God's command. Nineveh's testimony mirrors the prophet. They encountered much misery when they said "no" to God and wallowed in wickedness. Yet, when they repented and changed their ways, he withdrew his order of judgment and extended blessing in its place.

God has a way of doing things on a level far beyond our expectations. In the case of Jonah's obedience, God responded with an unbelievable miracle. In the most improbable city, filled with the most ungodly people, using the most unworthy of prophets, God sends a revival. In one day, an entire city repents and comes to God. No other revival in Scripture or throughout church history reports an entire city coming to God. Not only is the whole city saved, it is saved in one day! Obedience brings the most miraculous blessings to those who choose to exercise it.

When the books of the prophets are viewed in the light of the miraculous, most of us overlook Jonah. However, the account abounds with miracles. If we could flip on the TV and hear a panel of miracle analysts giving a breakdown of which miracle was greatest, I wonder what they would say. God created a storm that formed and dissipated on command, but that is not the greatest miracle. Jonah was swallowed whole by a great fish, but that is not the greatest miracle. He survived three days in fish's belly, but even that is not the greatest miracle in the story. I believe if we watched the show to the end, enduring all the pontificating and mindless commercial breaks, the panel would come to a consensus. The greatest miracle in the book of Jonah is that a whole city turned to God and was saved from destruction in response to the preaching of a half-hearted prophet. What a miracle!

Greatness in a man or woman can hardly be apprised, much less created. Yet, the book of Jonah contains the story of perhaps the greatest revival in the history of the world. Was Jonah the greatest prophet? Surely not, but through him, God did a great thing. We all desire to see God do great things in our homes, our churches, our communities, and our nation, but how will they come about? The answer is found in Jonah. Great things happen when average people obey their Great God. The question you must ask yourself is simple.

"What is God calling me to do?"

I do not know what caused you to pick up this book. Perhaps, you wanted another eschatological thriller. Maybe, you have a concern for your nation. Perhaps, you are a believer, but maybe you are not. That said, I do not know what the difficulty is in your life, nor the condition of your soul. But, I do know that whatever your current status, and whatever you may be struggling with, the answer can be found in Jesus. This world will soon pass away, and all that goes with it. Do not waste your life on things that have no eternal consequence, and do not give up on the purpose to which God has called you. The signs are clear, Jesus is coming soon. Are you ready?

NOTES

CHAPTER 1

1. *Mayflower Compact.* Chronology of U.S. Historical Documents. University of Oklahoma Law Center. 28 March, 1999 <http://www.law.ou.edu/hist/mayflow.html>.
2. Bob Klingenberg, *Is God with America*, (Maitland, Florida: Xulon Press, 2006), 208.
3. Leon G Stevens, *One Nation Under God*, (Bloomington, IN: Morgan James Publishing, 2013), 64.
4. Gerhard Peters and John T. Woolley, *George Washington: "Inaugural Address," April 30, 1789,* (The American Presidency Project. http://www.presidency.ucsb.edu/ws/?pid=25800).

5. General Orders (2 May 1778) published in *Writings of George Washington* (1932), Vol XI, 342-343.
6. William J. Federer, *America's God and Country* (St. Louis: Amerisearch; revised edition 2000), 669.
7. Kay Dee Lilley, *God's Country: America's Heart Cry*, (Maitland, FL: Xulon Press, 2010), 17.
8. Federer, 18.
9. Craig A Williams, Is there Evidence for the Christian Faith, (Maitland, FL: Xulon Press, 2001), 104.
10. Abraham Lincoln, *President Lincoln's Farewell Address, Springfield, Illinois, 1861*, Retrieved from the Library of Congress, <www.loc.gov/item/scsm000845/>.
11. Julian P. Boyd, Charles T. Cullen, John Catanzariti, Barbara B. Oberg, et al, eds, *The Papers of Thomas Jefferson*, (Princeton: Princeton University Press, 1950), 33 vols.
12. Woodrow Wilson, "The Road Away From Revolution," The Atlantic Monthly, August 1923: 145-146.
13. Franklin D. Roosevelt, Radio Address on Brotherhood Day, February 23, 1936.

Chapter 2

1. George Bancroft, *History of the United States*, (New York: D Appleton And Company, 1888).

2. Michael G. Long, *Billy Graham and the Beloved Community: America's Evangelist and the Dream of Martin Luther King, Jr.*, (New York: Palgrave Macmillan; First edition, 2006), 66.

Chapter 3

1. *Novanglus, and Massachusettensis: Political Essays, Published in the Years 1774 and 1775, on the Principal Points of Controversy, between Great Britain and Her Colonies,* (Boston: Hews and Goss, 1819).
2. A.J. Langguth, *Union 1812: The Americans Who Fought the Second War of Independence,* (New York: Simon & Schuster, 2006), 308-311.

Chapter 4

1. David Rolfs, *No Peace for the Wicked,* (Knoxville, TN: University of Tennessee Press; 1st edition (May 10, 2009), 141.
2. David Josiah Brewer, *The United States a Christian Nation,* (Philadelphia: John D. Winston Company, 1905), 23.
3. Ray Harker, *God in Government: The Christian's Guide to Civic Responsibility and Political Ideology,* (Indianapolis: Dog Ear Publishing, LLC, 2010), 70.
4. John R. Vile, *The Constitutional Convention of 1787,* (Denver: ABC-CLIO, 2005), 593.

5. Ed Imparato, General MacArthur: Wisdom and Visions, (Paducah, KY: Turner Publishing Company, 2001), 129.

Chapter 7

1. John Foxe, *Book of Martyrs: A Universal History of Christian Martyrdom from the Birth of Our Blessed Saviour to the Latest Periods of Persecution, Volumes 1-2,* (Cambridge: E. C. Biddle, 1840), 233.